Edgar Lee Masters

Twayne's United States Authors Series

David J. Nordloh, Editor

Indiana University, Bloomington

TUSAS 456

Edgar Lee Masters "about 33 years of age."
Photograph reproduced from Hardin W. Masters,
Edgar Lee Masters: A Centenary Memoir-Anthology
(South Brunswick and New York: A.S. Barnes and Co.).
Courtesy of Matzene Studio.

Edgar Lee Masters

By John H. Wrenn
and Margaret M. Wrenn

University of Colorado

Twayne Publishers • *Boston*

Edgar Lee Masters

John H. Wrenn
Margaret M. Wrenn

Copyright © 1983 by G. K. Hall & Company
All Rights Reserved
Published by Twayne Publishers
A Division of G. K. Hall & Company
70 Lincoln Street
Boston, Massachusetts 02111

Book Production by Marne B. Sultz

Book Design by Barbara Anderson

Printed on permanent/durable acid-free
paper and bound in the United States of
America.

Library of Congress Cataloging in Publication Data

Wrenn, John H.
Edgar Lee Masters.

(Twayne's United States authors series ; TUSAS 456)
Bibliography: p. 131
Includes index.
1. Masters, Edgar Lee, 1868–1950—Criticism and
interpretation.   I. Wrenn, Margaret M.   II. Title.
III. Series.
PS3529.A83Z88   1983   811'.52   83-10819
ISBN 0-8057-7396-7

For Catherine B. Wrenn,
our coauthor and best friend

Contents

About the Authors
Preface
Chronology

Chapter One
The Mystical and the Real   1

Chapter Two
The Macrocosm: History and Literature   14

Chapter Three
Chicago: The Way to Spoon River   22

Chapter Four
Widening Horizons:
Literary Friends and Influences   34

Chapter Five
Spoon River Anthology   45

Chapter Six
Spoon River Before and After:
Sources and Criticism   58

Chapter Seven
Other Directions in Poetry   68

Chapter Eight
Spoon River into Fiction   81

Chapter Nine
Biography: Setting the Record Straight   101

Chapter Ten
Across Spoon River   112

Notes and References   125
Selected Bibliography   131
Index   138

About the Authors

Margaret M. Wrenn received her B.A. in English from the University of Colorado. She has served as director of Renewable Resources in the Office of Energy Conservation for the State of Colorado, and has published numerous articles on solar energy and represented Colorado on a number of national boards and conferences. She is now Energy Program Director for the city of Boulder. Her father, John H. Wrenn, is a professor of English at the University of Colorado. He has published a book on John Dos Passos and served for a number of years as director of the Writers' Conference at the university. He earlier received a master's degree in English from the University of Michigan in Ann Arbor, and a doctoral degree in American civilization from the University of Pennsylvania. At present Professor Wrenn is working on a second edition of his Dos Passos volume and is editing a volume of contemporary reviews of Dos Passos's writing.

Preface

Sixty years ago Edgar Lee Masters (1868–1950) was America's best-known poet and, with the exception of Yeats, the most celebrated poet then living. Now, thirty years after his death, he is virtually forgotten, and today's students do not even recognize his name.

However, mention of the *Spoon River Anthology* (1914–15) may evoke a glimmer of recognition. Many will know the title only in its adaptation for stage presentation, but it will at least have the sound of a familiar name. For Spoon River, the town that never was, lives on, though the name of its inventor is no longer current. Yet Masters also published seven novels, sixteen plays and other dramatic works, numerous biographies, narrative and dramatic poems and collections of poems, histories, and essays. Of this impressive output only the *Anthology* is likely to have significant readership in the future. Already its most striking and memorable poems, such as "Fiddler Jones," "Anne Rutledge," and "Lucinda Matlock," have been dropped from the newer anthologies.

Nevertheless, the intrinsic qualities of the poetry remain, the same qualities that helped to make *Spoon River Anthology* in its time the best-known work of the American poetic renaissance of 1911–16, and Masters a chief spokesman for what was called the "new poetry." The fascinating puzzle which Masters presents is how to explain, first, the extraordinary reception of the Spoon River poems and their later neglect and, second, the unquestioned superiority of the *Anthology,* which stands head and shoulders above his many other publications.

Did Masters cease being a true poet with the publication of *Spoon River Anthology?* Was his later work different in kind or substance from his major book? Did success ruin him, as one myth would have it? Was he a plagiarist who stole the poems of the *Anthology* from another, unknown writer, as another myth has insisted? Or has American poetic taste undergone rapid and substantial change, and if so, how do we account for that change and what is its nature? And what of the author? What sort of man was he?

What is finally significant and interesting in a critical account of any artist is not what he has to say, for which we go directly to his work, nor even his account of himself—fortunately Masters, like many writers, gives a fairly full account of himself, particularly in the autobiography *Across Spoon River* (1936). The really interesting thing is the discovery of relationships. The poet virtually by definition leads the examined life, so in a sense it is unimportant which poet we select for scrutiny; in different lives and works we discern differing kinds and intensities of relationships. Yet the career of Edgar Lee Masters has its peculiar attractions. In few other writers are combined the romantic idealism and mysticism on the one hand and the lawyer's practical skepticism on the other. And no other American literary work has received such immediate and widespread popular and critical attention as that attracted to *Spoon River Anthology* when it first appeared in 1914–15.

The heartland of America has produced other spokesmen: Mark Twain and Abraham Lincoln, when it was still the West; the novelist Edward Eggleston (1837–1902) and poet James Whitcomb Riley (1849–1916), both celebrating Indiana village virtues; Vachel Lindsay (1879–1931) and Carl Sandburg (1878–1967), Illinois contemporaries with whom Masters was for so long linked in poetry anthologies. Yet no other American writer has seemed to feel in his bones with such intensity as Masters the attraction and repulsion of the urban and rural Midwest, of the great continental drainage basin which is a central though seldom acknowledged factor in the psychology and culture of America. Now, a third of a century after his death, we have the perspective from which we can begin to assess the importance of Edgar Lee Masters as a spokesman for his place and time, and of *Spoon River Anthology* in American literary history.

In probing these relationships, we discover familiar and unfamiliar names in a list of remarkable men and women. Among them are earlier poets, Whitman, Shelley, Goethe, and contemporary writers who were Masters's close friends, Theodore Dreiser, Carl Sandburg, and H. L. Mencken. There is Ezra Pound, who for a moment hailed Masters as the true American poet; and there are the editors Harriet Monroe of Chicago's *Poetry* magazine, his steadfast supporter, and

William Marion Reedy, who first published the Spoon River poems in his literary newspaper, the *Mirror*.

We discover strong threads of relationship to the dominating figures of the Mississippi Valley, Lincoln and Twain, both of whom Masters worshipped and then denied in denigrating biographies. Here are the names of Clarence Darrow, Masters's Chicago law partner, whose novel *Farmington* (1904) anticipated *Spoon River,* and Masters's early political idol William Jennings Bryan—these two, Darrow and Bryan, later to meet as adversaries in the Scopes Trial concerning the teaching of evolution in Tennessee.

Among the many women in his life those who represent important strands in the skein of relationships are not, interestingly, his mother, his sister, or either of his two wives. They are rather his grandmother Masters, who sat for the verse portrait "Lucinda Matlock"; the liberated feminist, musician, and sculptor Tennessee Mitchell, whom he loved passionately and who later became the wife of Sherwood Anderson; and Alice Davis, his friend and companion during his most productive years in New York City.

The literary archeologist who picks a site or subject for a "dig" never knows what the probes may uncover. Choose a Midwestern site like Spoon River, Illinois, and slowly a line of village microcosms begins to emerge: Tilbury Town in Maine; Spoon River; Winesburg, Ohio; Yoknapatawpha County in Mississippi. Scrape away the alluvium of time, and the famous literary "revolt from the village" becomes visible as almost the reverse of what we had thought. Similarly, beneath the hardened mask of the realistic cynic, we discover the gentler lineaments of a romantic optimist.

John H. Wrenn
Margaret M. Wrenn

University of Colorado

Chronology

1868   Edgar Lee Masters is born 23 August in Garnett, Kansas, son of Hardin W. Masters and Emma Dexter Masters.

1869   Masters family returns to the Illinois farm of Hardin's parents in Menard County near Petersburg.

1870–1880   Spends childhood in and around Petersburg, Illinois. Younger brother Alexander dies of diphtheria, age five, in 1878; best friend Mitch Miller dies 1879.

1880–1890   Family moves to Lewistown, Illinois. Masters attends Lewistown high school, graduating 1886. Publishes his first writing in *Chicago Daily News* and elsewhere. Works in his father's law office.

1891–1892   Admitted to the Illinois Bar. Moves to Chicago. Works as bill collector for Edison Company. Meets Ernest McGaffey.

1893   Establishes first law office in Chicago with Kicksham Scanlon. Writes play *Benedict Arnold*.

1898   *A Book of Verses*. 21 June, marries Helen Jenkins.

1899   Son, Hardin Masters, born.

1900–1902   "The Constitution and Our Insular Possessions"; *Maximillian*, play; articles in *Chicago Chronicle*.

1903–1908   Law partnership with Clarence Darrow. Two daughters, Madeline and Marcia, born. *New Star Chamber* (1904) collected from *Chronicle* articles. Plays, *The Blood of the Prophets* (1905), *Althea* (1907), *The Trifler* (1908).

1909   Play, *The Leaves of the Tree*. Affair with Tennessee Mitchell; wife refuses to divorce him.

1910   Plays, *Eileen* and *The Locket*. Publishes *Songs and Sonnets*, under pseudonym Webster Ford.

1911   Bitter end to partnership with Clarence Darrow; sets up private law practice. Ends affair with Tennessee Mitchell. Play, *The Bread of Idleness*.

1912   *Songs and Sonnets, Second Series*.

1914   29 May, first "Spoon River" epitaphs appear pseudonymously in Reedy's *Mirror*. November, Masters reveals authorship.

1915   *Spoon River Anthology* in book form. January, pneumonia.

1916   Helen Haire Levinson Prize awarded by *Poetry* magazine. *The Great Valley* and *Songs and Satires*, poems, and new edition of *Spoon River Anthology* with thirty-two new poems.

1917–1919   Leaves wife and family. *Toward the Gulf* (1918) and *Starved Rock* (1919), poems.

1920   Gives up law practice and moves to New York. *Domesday Book*, long poetic narrative, and *Mitch Miller*, novel for boys.

1921   *The Open Sea*, poems. Trip to Europe. Wife begins divorce litigation (1921–23), represented by Clarence Darrow.

1922   *Children of the Marketplace, A Fictitious Autobiography*, biography of Stephen A. Douglas.

1923   *The Nuptial Flight*, novel, and *Skeeters Kirby*, sequel to *Mitch Miller*. Final divorce decree.

1924   *Mirage*, sequel to *Skeeters Kirby*; *The New Spoon River*, collection of poems in the original "Spoon River" vein.

1925   *Selected Poems*. Extensive lecture tour; taking notes for "The New Atlantis" (*The New World*).

1926   *Lee, A Dramatic Poem*. Marries Ellen Coyne, thirty years his junior.

1927   *Kit O'Brien*, boys' book, and *Levy Mayer and the New Industrial Era*, biography.

1928   *Jack Kelso, A Dramatic Poem*. Son, Hilary Masters, born to Ellen Coyne Masters. Father, Hardin Masters, dies.

1929   *Fate of the Jury*, epilogue to *Domesday Book*.

1930   *Lichee Nuts*, poems, and *Gettysburg, Manila, Ácoma*, dramatic poetry.

1931   *Godbey, A Dramatic Poem*, sequel to *Jack Kelso*, and *Lincoln: The Man*, biography.

1932–1934   *The Tale of Chicago* (1933), history; *The Serpent in the Wilderness* (1933), poems; plays, *Moroni, Richmond*; four *Dramatic Duologues*.

1935   *Vachel Lindsay: A Poet in America*, biography, and *Invisible Landscapes*, poems.

1936   Autobiography, *Across Spoon River. The Golden Fleece of California*, poetic narrative, and *Poems of People*. Awarded Mark Twain silver medal.

1937   *The New World*, long narrative poem; *The Tide of Time*, novel; *Whitman*, biography.

1938   *Mark Twain: A Portrait*, biography.

1939   *More People*, poems. Coast-to-coast lecture tour.

1940   Edits *The Living Thoughts of Ralph Waldo Emerson*.

1941   Poetry Society of America Award. *Illinois Poems*.

1942   *Along the Illinois*, poetry, and *The Sangamon*, nonfiction for The Rivers of America Series. Grant from American Academy of Arts and Letters and National Institute of Arts and Letters.

1943–1949   Health deteriorates; end of Hotel Chelsea years. Shelley Memorial Award (1944); first $5,000 fellowship granted by Academy of American Poets (1946).

1950   Masters dies, 5 March, and is buried at Oakland Cemetery, Petersburg, Illinois.

Chapter One
The Mystical and the Real
Fate and the Stars

Edgar Lee Masters's autobiography, *Across Spoon River* (1936), reveals a strong sense of fate. In the early pages, speaking of a part of his heritage, Masters writes of the "strands of fate" apparent in his childhood, especially that of his affection for his grandmother.[1] Another strand, he notes, was his relationship with his sister, affected by his mother's partiality for her (*ASR*, 35). Later he speaks of regrettable circumstances arising from a "fateful" series of events (*ASR*, 63); more generally, he asserts that seeking "the eternal feminine" was "fated" in his nature (*ASR*, 170–71).

Finally, in the last pages of his book, in his discussion of the "clairvoyance" (*ASR*, 352) which he says accompanied the writing of the *Spoon River Anthology* (1915), Masters speaks of his continuing consciousness of a "good daemon" or "brother god" who would be his guide along the predestined fortunate ways (*ASR*, 399). This daemon first appears as a mystical star in "Elijah Browning," the penultimate poem in the *Spoon River Anthology*. The speaker from a mountain top touches the star and perceives "Infinite Truth." It next appears in "The Star," the final poem of *Songs and Satires* (1916). It finally is the star, Masters makes clear in the epilogue to *Across Spoon River,* the inescapable star that must be served but seemed to be not a star, after all, but Selene (the moon), and yet not that goddess but "my brother . . . god" in the form of the goddess (*ASR*, 415–16).

Masters's emphasis on fate, destiny, star, and predestination tempts us to examine his horoscope. That would seem to many an unscientific approach to criticism, and yet the scientific approach may not be the best or only fruitful approach to a poet. In his last novel, *The Tide of Time* (1937), Masters uses astrological reference to foreshadow the success of his protagonist, Leonard Atterberry, modeled

1

on the poet's father Hardin Masters: the sign of Leo at his birth presages courage and power in his life (17). In his critical study *Mark Twain* (1938), Masters writes that Twain in his last illness spoke of dual personality and perhaps realized the presence of a mysterious other world. He writes of the "prodigy" that Twain was born when Halley's comet was at its perihelion in 1835 and died when it returned in 1910 (237–38). Twain too had his "brother" star and confidently associated his own life with the period of Halley's Comet. As to the charge that astrological evidences are unscholarly, Masters, who considered himself a scholar, answers in the poem "The Search" from *The Great Valley* (1916), that "the scholar" sleeps outdoors "to study the Zodiac."

The starting point for biography and for horoscopy is the place and time of birth. Masters provides both in the first sentence of *Across Spoon River:* that he was born in Garnett, Kansas at 4:00 A.M., 23 August 1869. The precision of the hour is somewhat remarkable, especially in view of the facts that nothing more is made of it and that the *year* appears to be wrong. Kimball Flaccus, in a monograph devoted to Masters, notes that, "The year of [Masters's] birth is correctly stated as 1868, although it appears incorrectly in many works of reference as 1869. The error crept by chance into one of the editions of *Who's Who in America;* according to Mrs. Masters, her husband never bothered to correct it [for] it made him a year younger."[2]

A professional astrologer, having been given Masters's date, time, and place of birth but not his name, has provided "the detailed planetary and zodiacal pattern at the time and place of the birth of No Name." The astrologer interprets these calculations, without knowledge of the identity of the male subject: "This person has sun 0° in Virgo. Leo is rising at 13°, and his moon is 11° Scorpio. These are the three basic factors of the chart. They give a quick, composite sketch of what the person is like; what I would call the initials of the Zodiac name."[3] The calculations indicate to the professional reader a strong need for self-expression, a tendency toward conflict of wills, an inner restlessness, a concern for reform and social justice, a sense of destiny and mysticism combined with good luck. Of the four elements—earth, air, fire, and water—water predominates in the horoscope, fire is next, and air is missing.

These and other qualities inferred from the horoscope figure prominently, implicitly or explicitly, in Masters's work. They may provide useful clues toward an explanation of the phenomenon *Spoon River Anthology*. Whether from the configurations of planets and stars or from the circumstances of his environment, mysticism and a sense of destiny play an observable role in Masters's life and work, as do images of water and fire.

The central fact of *Spoon River Anthology* is that it is a book of the dead, a collection of epitaphs presumably engraved or to be engraved on gravestones. Masters was acquainted with death from his earliest years, much of it associated with water and fire. Before he was five years old, in 1873, he recalls in the autobiography, the nearby river overflowed and the waters rose to the Masters house. General sickness ensued, and a playmate, also named Lee, died of diphtheria. At about this time the house across the street caught fire. Fire and water, Masters says, make indelible imprints in the memory. Here he notes the birth of a younger brother, "beautiful as Shelley" (*ASR*, 25–26). Masters barely mentions these events in passing, yet the reader is struck by the probable effect on a five-year-old boy of the death of a playmate of his own age and name. The birth in the same year of his mystically beautiful and precocious brother must have seemed a simple replacement. However, this brother, Alexander Masters, died of diphtheria in September 1878, also at the age of five.

Late that same fall, in 1878, the grieving mother, Emma Masters, took her two surviving children to Leavenworth, Kansas, to visit her sister, who had herself recently lost her son by drowning in the Missouri River. With a mystical, unquestioning acceptance of the possibility of communing with the dead, Masters writes that his aunt was communing with her dead son, that she and his mother talked of spiritualism throughout the visit while the children listened in terror of ghosts (*ASR*, 43). Masters's best friend at this time was Mitch Miller, whom he much later memorialized in his novel for boys, *Mitch Miller* (1920). Within a year of the death of Masters's brother Alex, Mitch was dead, killed while hopping a freight train. During this same period the boy Masters, he tells us in *The Sangamon* (1942), was nearly drowned while fishing at the millrace at New Salem, about two miles from Petersburg (72–73).

All these deaths were pooled in the mystical imagination of Lee Masters with the death of Alex. Also identified with Alex is his Aunt Mary Masters, a lovely girl who was an invalid for seven years in his grandfather's farmhouse, whiling away the time reading Tennyson and Shelley (39). Mary Masters, incidentally, appears in Masters's novel *Nuptial Flight* (1923) as Lucy Houghton, who was "destined" to an unhappy life by the "inevitable influence" of the stars she was born under (145). Like Alex, the younger brother "beautiful as Shelley," Mary Masters was buried first at Petersburg and later removed to the family plots purchased in Oakland Cemetery near Petersburg. Neither, Masters was "horror-stricken" to observe (*ASR,* 39), ever had a memorial stone. His brother's first external memorial was the *Spoon River* poem "Hamlet Micure," in which he appears as "little Paul," somehow identified with "Alfred," Lord Tennyson. (Autobiographical details in another *Spoon River* epitaph reveal that the speaker of "Alfred Moir" is Masters; in Masters's novel *Nuptial Flight* the hero, who is Masters himself, is named Alfred.)

These mystical relationships are complicated in Masters's lifelong admiration for the poet Shelley, who is the "good daemon, a brother god," mentioned above, who is the star and "Eternal Love" of the poem, "The Star," and who is also the lost beautiful brother. A portion of the poem "Neanderthal" from *Toward the Gulf* (1918) asks of the poet Shelley why he comes "with veiled face" to guard the sleep of the speaker, when suddenly the speaker recognizes the no longer veiled face of "The god, my brother."

Here is the face "beautiful as Shelley" of his brother Alex, and of the invalid Mary Masters. Here is the brotherhood of the dead playmate who had borne his own name Lee, the brotherhood of Alex and of their first cousin who died by drowning, and of Mitch Miller. Here is the veil or caul, the removal of which signifies life, as when he reports the event in the first paragraph of his autobiography—his grandmother "lifted the veil" from his face on his arrival at the Petersburg farm in 1869.

In addition to these early impingements of death were the winter cold and sickness Masters recalled from these years, in *Across Spoon River,* and the summer terror of lightning storms (another fire image) and cyclones: one lightning bolt knocked down the boy Lee as he was playing and badly burned his cousin Daisy (*ASR,* 31), who died about a year later; during Masters's last summer in Petersburg the grandparents' farm was nearly destroyed by a cyclone (*ASR,* 50). These are memories of a harsh and often pitiless environment.

The Great River Valley

After eleven years in the area of Petersburg on the Sangamon River, the family moved to Lewistown on the Spoon. The chief geographical feature of the central Illinois region where Masters grew up is of course the great continental drainage basin of the Mississippi River, which is itself a dominant water image in the American literary consciousness. Of Masters's many titles referring to water, both *The Great Valley* (1916) and *Toward the Gulf* indicate the force of the Mississippi image in his own consciousness.

Although the Mississippi forms the western boundary of Illinois separating that state from Missouri, it dominates the interior of both states by virtue of their principal rivers, the Illinois and the Missouri, both of which empty into the Mississippi at the great bend of the river above East St. Louis, Illinois. The Illinois River arises in the extreme north of the state, in the Great Lakes area of Chicago, on the shores of Lake Michigan. In almost the exact center of the state is the Sangamon, flowing south and west toward the capital, Springfield, then west and north past new Salem, where Lincoln lived, and past Masters's Petersburg, and finally west into the Illinois, ninety to a hundred miles north of the confluence of the Illinois with the Mississippi. Some twenty miles northeast of the junction of the Sangamon with the Illinois, the Spoon River flows south and east past Lewistown to join the Illinois at Havana.

The river which overflowed and brought flood, diphtheria, and death to young Lee Masters's consciousness and in which he himself nearly drowned at the millrace was the Sangamon. Masters compared it to the Mississippi, as he and his friend Mitch Miller relived the adventures of Tom Sawyer and Huck Finn. The fearsome, ice-clogged river he crossed with his sister and mother on their trip to Leavenworth, Kansas, after young Alex Masters died, was the Mississippi. The river in which his cousin had drowned at Leavenworth was the Missouri. The river that Masters made famous was the Spoon. To the boy Masters of course the rivers were parts of the natural environment. The Mississippi Valley, in association with death and mysticism, remained in his mind and memory a controlling image and source of inspiration.

Home and Family

The two towns in which Masters grew up represented to him conflicting values: Petersburg stood for his father and the agrarian culture of the South, Lewistown for his mother and the village morality of her New England background. Together they made up his early Midwest heritage. Although he took his Illinois childhood environment for granted, he became increasingly conscious of his Midwest identity as he grew into manhood. When he arrived in Chicago in 1892, when it had already become the Midwestern metropolis and was preparing for the Columbian Exposition or World's Fair, Masters was well on his way to complete identification with the Midwest as his proper soil, as the raw material for his creative work, and as his spiritual home.

There is a kind of dualism native to the Midwest affecting its psychology. The Midwest is peopled by settlers from the Northeast and from the South, yet it offers these people an identity which is neither Northern nor Southern, Eastern nor Western. The settlers of Illinois, for example, were of diverse origins ranging from Virginia and Tennessee to the New England states. These settlers usually maintained their Northern or Southern identities through a generation or more before they succumbed to the fusion of the Midwest locale, and even today there are some towns which remain distinctively either "Northern" or "Southern."

Social critics have observed that Midwest literature is often imbued with "a strain of double feeling," a paradoxical dichotomy of North and South, illusion and disillusion, fusion and friction created by the diversity of the people and of elements in the locale. Max Lerner points out that the Midwest dualism may result largely from "the decisive part that the Midwest played in the Civil War, which may even be viewed as a struggle between North and South to control the future development of the Midwestern area."[4] This Midwest dualism has been a source of creative tension for much of America's Midwestern literature, and is epitomized by the contrasting shore and raft psychologies in the fictional masterpiece of the area, Mark Twain's *The Adventures of Huckleberry Finn* (1885).

The same dualism, traceable to the conflicts implicit in Masters's heredity and locale, permeates his work. In "The Genesis of Spoon River" (1933), he notes that when he was about eleven he and his family moved north to Lewistown within five miles of the Spoon, where New England Calvinism was engaged in a "death struggle" with the "free livers" of Virginia. Lewistown to Masters was northern and puritanical, while Petersburg, fifty miles south, was southern and genially free.[5]

Across Spoon River is filled with idealized accounts of Masters's father's Petersburg family from Virginia and Tennessee. His mother's puritanical New England family he regarded much less cordially. They represented to him (although he never knew them) the moralistic, blue-nosed, prohibitionist bigots of the North, from whom his mother inherited her willfulness (10).

The young Edgar Lee, or Lee, as he was generally called, obviously sympathized more with his struggling father than he did with his mother. Hardin Masters worked long hours successively as grocer, school teacher, and lawyer to provide for his growing family, while Emma never had the meals on time or managed to keep the house orderly and comfortable (12).

Masters loved his father and admired him for his vitality and easy sociability, for his outspoken liberalism and his great strength, which he credited to his father's stalwart pioneer-farmer heritage. These Southern-born qualities in his father were to him among the most desirable "American" qualities. He took to his heart the Southern ideal of Jeffersonian agrarianism his father's heritage reflected: hearty individualism graced with humble industry and hard work. Masters quite early in life adopted Jeffersonian Democracy as his political and social creed. He followed in his father's professional footsteps to become a lawyer who characteristically fought for the poor, for labor, for increased electoral and state powers, and against narrow moralities, against prohibition, against big money and corporation interests. He later dedicated his *Domesday Book* (1920) to his father as one of the last of "A Passing Species—An American."

As for his mother, Masters both hated and loved her at the same time, as if by the same impulse. The *New Spoon River* (1924) he dedicated "To / My Mother / Emma J. Masters." But one wonders if the dedication was in part a reaction against the hateful picture he had painted of his mother (who was still living—she died in 1926) as Fanny Houghton in *Nuptial Flight* (1923). In this novel Masters fictionalized with very little artistic detachment his own family and their fates. Fanny Houghton he characterized as an unbelievably selfish, willful termagant of a woman from New England who marries and nearly destroys Walter Scott Houghton, a handsome, likable man of Southern stock. In the novel Masters blames the disintegrated lives of two generations of Houghtons chiefly on Fanny's frustrated nature and querulous personality. The end of the novel shows all the principal characters, including the artistic son

Alfred—the hero, a very slightly masked Edgar Lee—as broken, disillusioned, disintegrated personalities who return (all but the intransigent Fanny) to the grandparents' farm as a final haven from the world.

Although he fictionalized her in *Nuptial Flight* as an incredible virago, Masters shows elsewhere some understanding of his mother. He saw his parents' marriage as the struggle of two indomitable wills. Their marriage was a joining of New England's "gospel hate" and the South's "gospel love" (*ASR*, 10). But he supposes that his father might have been better prepared for the responsibility of a wife and family, and he understands that his mother, still very young when she married, was subjected to hardships she was unequipped for in a land she hated till the end (*ASR*, 10–11). She never felt at home in this bare, desolate, uncivilized country, as she conceived it. And she was never able to make a home there for her family, driving Lee, her oldest son, to repeated escapes to the domesticity and affection of his grandmother and finally entirely away from the village of Lewistown to Chicago.

Yet in many respects Masters even admired and respected his mother. He recognized her intelligence and perceptivity. He especially noted her flashing "divinations," her "clairvoyant eyes" (*ASR*, 338). "The humor, the characterization, the lusty vitality" of the Spoon River portraits were from his father, and "the philosophy, the mysticism, the imagery," and the irony were from his mother, their democracy from him, their doubt of it from her; "their passion and vitality" came from both.[6]

A careful reading of *Across Spoon River* shows the importance of Masters's mother in his development. His ambivalence, his alternating attraction and repulsion toward her, are evidence that he felt the power of her presence. Whereas Masters's father discouraged his son from literary pursuits and encouraged him to more practical reading of law, Masters's mother loved literature and spent many hours with her son Edgar Lee and his sister Madeline in reading and comparing their own compositions.

If the relationship between his parents was one kind of conflict, Masters saw the difference in cultures between Petersburg and Lewistown, the towns in which he spent his formative years, as another. The first eleven of these years he lived near his grandparents in Petersburg, Southern-rural, agrarian, Jeffersonian-democratic. The next eleven he spent in Lewistown, settled mainly by New Englanders, urban, mercantile, Calvinist-prohibitionist. Lewistown provided the adolescent Masters with many inferences, accurate and inaccurate, about his mother's birthplace. He wrote of the slovenly men and women of Lewistown, fighting, tobacco-spitting beasts catered to by miserly merchants, in contrast to his elegant, kindly grandparents, who patronized the better shops in Petersburg. He remarks that he survived Lewistown's dangers unharmed, but changed in point of view (*ASR*, 410–11).

Whatever injury Masters incurred from living in Lewistown turned out to be a great asset, at least in terms of his literary career. The way it affected his outlook was to disillusion him, to show him the other side of the Midwestern coin from what became by contrast his idyllic image of Petersburg. His memory of Petersburg was especially nostalgic because it was most removed from him in time, because it represented the farm as opposed to the village, or perhaps the town as opposed to the village. In an odd reversal of customary emphasis Masters used the term "village" most often in a derogatory sense as in "village ignorance" (*ASR*, 80). But he usually referred to Petersburg as a "town": "one of the most attractive towns in Illinois," "a town like Petersburg."[7]

Petersburg represented to Masters, then, the town as opposed to the village (Lewistown), agrarianism as opposed to industrialism, and old-time Southern dignity as opposed to modern industrial money-grubbing. It provided the emotional base for his politics as a Jeffersonian Democrat, for his retrospective farm romanticism, for his belief in states' rights and agrarianism as opposed to industrialist imperialism. It offered him models, very nearly the only ones in his experience, of people living happily—Midwesterners from Southern stock, farmers, Democrats, anti-Calvinists. Writing of the Petersburg area as late as his seventy-third year, he said that the country still appealed to him as strongly as ever and remained fresh in his imagination, to "the very accent" of the people's words.[8]

Together Petersburg and Lewistown provided Masters with the dramatic tension which inspired most of his fifty-odd volumes. Most notably they became the imaginary town Spoon River with its conflicting ideas and actualities, hopes and achievements, exalted spirits and wasted lives. The progression in Masters's life and mind from farm to small town to semi-industrialized "village" (and finally to the urban metropolis of Chicago) is a fairly obvious one. It was a northerly progression away from the Virginia-Tennessee antecedents that Masters cherished in his paternal background. It was upstream from Concord Creek and the Sangamon to the Spoon, to Lake Michigan and the upper Illinois River. It was out of eighteenth-century rural America into twentieth-century urban-industrial America. It was out of the womb, the heaven-haven of the grandmaternal homestead, and into the world of childhood and adolescence, of pain and loss, and finally to the anonymity of the mass in Chicago.

Growing and Becoming

Meanwhile the farm, Petersburg, and Lewistown were consolidating their effects, molding the man, particularly through education, personal relationships, and the development of his will. Masters thought of himself, as he wrote in characteristic candor toward the end of his autobiography, as ruled by his will and by "selfish passion" (*ASR*, 405). By "selfish passion" he meant that erotic pursuit of women that he conceived was fated in his nature (*ASR*, 170–71). By his "will" he meant also the exercise of his inherited or "fated" will—an "exhaustless, continuous energy" he felt he had inherited from his grandmother Masters (*ASR*, 402).

It is clear that his grandmother Lucinda Masters was a dominant influence in his career, particularly in these early years. She is the "Lucinda Matlock" of one of the most famous of his *Spoon River* epitaphs. She remained inseparable in his mind from the tone and ambience of the farm and Petersburg. The boy Lee spent as much time as possible in her company at the farm, devouring the family's library, largely illustrated children's books (*ASR*, 19). Yet every time he visited the farm it was against the will of his mother, who was jealous of his grandmother's influence on the boy. Lee was proud to be the favorite grandchild; he was even proud to learn, after he became a man, that his grandmother was an illegitimate child (*ASR*, 6–7), raised by her mother's parents (Masters's great-great-grandparents) John and Rebecca Wasson, who appear as separate portraits under their own names in *Spoon River Anthology*.

Of next importance among his family, after his parents, his grandmother, and his young brother Alex—the "boy beautiful as Shelley" who died when Lee was ten—was his sister Madeline, two years his junior. Of her he writes that despite her wealth in later years she never assisted him, but rather at critical times was a distinct hindrance (*ASR*, 20).

A second brother, Thomas Davis, was born shortly after Alex and Mitch Miller died. Masters refers to him as Davis in *Skeeters Kirby* (1923), the sequel to his book for boys, *Mitch Miller*. In both books Kirby is Masters himself. Masters tells in *Skeeters Kirby* of Mrs. Miller and Mrs. Kirby giving birth to baby boys shortly after the deaths of Mitch and "Little Billy," as Alex is called in these books. Of the Miller baby, Skeeters remarks that its arrival made it seem "as if God meant to send somebody" to replace Mitch. But no one could replace Mitch for his friend Skeeters, so "it seemed all wrong to me for [him] to be born." And then he comments that his mother too had been given a child, Davis, who "didn't die like [the Miller baby] did" (16–17). Masters's attitude toward his brother Tom seems to be close to that of Skeeters toward these two "replacements." Masters considered Tom a liability.

Of more importance than his surviving siblings, even in these pre-Chicago years, were his "chum" (as he everywhere calls him), Mitch Miller; his teacher, Mary Fisher; and Margaret George, a girl of his own age in Lewistown. Mitch is the hero of the eleven childhood years in Petersburg and the hero of the first book of Masters's fictional autobiographical trilogy, *Mitch Miller, Skeeters Kirby,* and *Mirage* (1924). Masters is Kirby throughout, the narrator of the first two books and the hero of the second and third. Mary Fisher and Margaret George are the joint heroines of the eleven adolescent years in Lewistown.

Mary Fisher was Masters's teacher in the high school in Lewistown. She was unusually well read and well prepared as a teacher. Masters tells of his inspiration by this remarkable teacher (*ASR,* 59) and of his introduction to the classics of English and American literature. Chief among the latter for Masters was Emerson, whose essays he bought by mail and read enthusiastically, as he wrote in one of his last books, an edition of Emerson.[9] Miss Fisher also introduced her charges to contemporary poets such as Eugene Field, an important Illinois poet in the 1880s. In view of his later work, it is of some interest that Masters soon after finishing high school was submitting poems of his own to Eugene Field's poetry column in the *Chicago Record* (*ASR,* 100).

Also contributing to Field's column at this time, about 1887–88, when Masters was nineteen or twenty, was Margaret Gilman George, a talented young woman, the daughter of the Presbyterian minister of Lewistown. She also had come under the influence of

Miss Fisher, though she had not attended the high school from which Masters graduated in 1886 with an oration on Robert Burns. A damaged heart valve restricted her activities so that she was tutored at home, where she had read widely in her father's extensive library. This library became available to Masters as did the instruction of her father, who taught him Latin.

Masters's relationship with Margaret (whom he calls by her sister's name, Anne, in *Across Spoon River*) seems to have been an intellectual and idealistic one. They had each heard of the other's accomplishments in reading and writing and so were attracted to one another. He decided that he really ought to be in love with the girl; so he deliberately fell in love, as he lamented later (*ASR,* 90). His thinking that he ought to be in love was related not to social pressures, but rather to his adolescent concept of appropriate behavior for a romantic poet, a notion he derived from reading Shelley. He had bought a handsome edition of Shelley's poems, and Shelley's humanitarian enthusiasm opened up to him whole new vistas in which he should find for himself a companion of physical and intellectual beauty (*ASR,* 77, 87–88). He deliberately sought out Margaret George in pursuance of this Shelleyan ideal, and he willed himself to fall in love with her.

Masters has presented his relationship with Margaret George most fully in *Skeeters Kirby,* where he calls her Winifred Henry. In both *Across Spoon River* and the fiction, she is a major force in the life of the protagonist, offering him love and encouragement in his desire for learning and his interest in writing. In the novel their relationship is terminated only by Winifred's untimely death from a heart ailment within a year or two of their meeting. In the nonfiction Masters says that he asserted himself and ended the affair (*ASR,* 102). In both works Masters's father is strongly opposed to the liaison, to the prohibitionist activities of Margaret's pastor father, and to Masters's spending himself in his literary ambitions when he might have been preparing to join his father in the practice of law. Between his father's will and Margaret George's love, Masters says, he was molded and matured (*ASR,* 88).

During these Lewistown years Hardin Masters acceded to his son's wishes to the extent of sending him for a year (1889–90) to Knox College in Galesburg, Illinois. Because of the random and heterogeneous nature of his studies, in which he was largely self-taught, Masters was unable to matriculate as a freshman, though he spent a happy year there as a student. Following his year at Knox College, he was forced to accede in turn to his father's wishes: he taught school (as unsuccessfully as his father before him) for three months; he read law and helped his father in his law office; he was admitted to the bar, made a false start at independence in Minneapolis-St. Paul, and returned to a brief partnership with his father in 1891. This was his last year living at home in Lewistown. Finally, after an argument with his mother over some literary matter, she vigorously asserted her will by knocking her son on the head with a rolled-up window shade. Masters thereupon asserted his own will by packing up and leaving for Chicago. Even if he had known that Chicago would kill him within six months, he would have been no less determined to leave (*ASR*, 135). Chicago would be the larger center of his activities for his second twenty-two years.

Chapter Two
The Macrocosm: History and Literature
The Tide of Intellectual Events

While Masters was growing up in the microcosmic villages of Petersburg-Lewistown, events were transpiring in the world at large which had their inevitable effects on the man he became. The importance in his family of the Civil War, which ended three years before his birth, has already been indicated.

Charles Darwin's *Origin of the Species*, published in that remarkable year for English literature, 1859, a decade before Masters's birth, affected Western civilization of his and subsequent generations. Especially through the writings of Darwin's disciple Herbert Spencer, Americans developed from the theory of evolution two somewhat opposed attitudes. One was an optimistic belief in inevitable progress, including the physical and moral improvement of man. The other was the pessimistic view of American literary naturalism—as expressed for example in the novels of Masters's friend Theodore Dreiser—that man is controlled by biological and other natural forces that deny him a say in his destiny. Both attitudes appear throughout Masters's work. An interesting collateral event is the birth in 1857, two years before Darwin's book appeared, of Clarence Darrow. Darrow was later to become Masters's law partner for eight years, then his enemy, and later still the defense lawyer upholding the evolutionary view in the famous Scopes Trial of 1925.

In that same year 1859 (in which Thomas Macaulay, Leigh Hunt, and Thomas DeQuincey died and in which Arthur Conan Doyle and the poet Francis Thompson were born) John Stuart Mill published his essay *On Liberty,* which eventually affected the political and legal thought of even such unnoted libertarians as the Illinois attorneys Hardin Masters and his son Edgar Lee. In 1859 a classical scholar and poet, Edward FitzGerald, published an enormously popular collection of pessimistic nostalgic lyrics, the *Rubaiyat of Omar Khayyam*. In 1858 A. E. Housman was born, later also to become a classical scholar and poet, and author of a remarkably popular volume of short, pessimistic poems of ordinary country and village folk, *A Shropshire Lad* (1896). Both anticipated the classical scholarship and pessimistic world view behind Masters's *Spoon River Anthology*. Housman's book, in fact, and even one particular poem, "Is My Team Plowing?" may be a primary source of Masters's *Anthology*. Spoken from the grave in an ironic dialogue, the poem begins, " 'Is my team ploughing, / That I was used to drive . . . ?' " Masters's epitaph "Hare Drummer" begins in a similar questioning rhythm, asking if the young people "still go to Siever's" to get apple cider in the afternoons.

In 1858, Alfred Tennyson published his *Idylls of the King*, a source of some of Masters's early verse based on Arthurian legends. In America in 1858 Mrs. Stowe published *The Minister's Wooing*, a novel which anticipated Masters's work in its regionalism and its anti-Calvinism (as well as in its interest in a romance between an older man and a younger woman, an autobiographical plot element common in Masters).

Of these literary events a decade before Masters's birth, only the work of Darwin, Housman, and Tennyson may have demonstrably affected Masters's thought and writing. Yet all of these indicate something of the literary and intellectual currents in "the tide of time" (to borrow the title phrase of his late novel) into which he was born. Other events of his birth year and later have a similar interest in their relation to his career. In the year Masters was born, 1868, for example, Robert Browning published *The Ring and the Book*, a novelistic poem told in blank-verse dramatic monologues much like Masters's *Domesday Book* and its sequel *The Fate of the Jury* (1929). Masters may well have sketched his own story, as he claims, as early as 1889 (the year Browning died), long before he read Browning's poem (*ASR,* 369); yet his admiration for Browning is evident in his "Browning as a Philosopher," a paper he read to the Chicago Literary Club in 1912, and perhaps in his adaptation of the dramatic monologue in *Spoon River Anthology*.

In 1868 New York State passed its Comstock Law, forerunner of the federal law five years later, by which Anthony Comstock persuaded citizens to legislate "the suppression of the trade in and circulation of obscene literature." Comstockery, as a residuum of Calvinism, Masters opposed throughout his life, in the *Spoon River Anthology* and elsewhere. The sexual frankness of his Spoon River people was partially responsible for the success as well as for the notoriety of his *Anthology*.

In 1869 Edwin Arlington Robinson was born. By the following year both Robinson and Masters had arrived in the areas they would later make famous in verse: Gardiner, Maine, Robinson's Tilbury Town, and Petersburg, Masters's Spoon River. In this year 1869 the transcontinental railroad was completed and the Suez Canal opened, events which signaled to Walt Whitman, in "Passage to India," the unity of America and the world. Whitman was working on the fifth edition of his *Leaves of Grass* (1855–71), to which Masters's *Spoon River Anthology* was to be indebted both for its free verse and its occasional colloquial idiom. In fact, as Masters wrote concerning his own later biography *Whitman* (1937), an early critic of *Spoon River Anthology* in 1915 had called Masters "the natural child of Walt Whitman." Furthermore Masters had long admired Whitman, especially for his patriotic vision, and in his first book, *A Book of Verses* (1898), he had praised Whitman. [1]

Crosscurrents: The 1870s and 1880s

In 1871, when Masters was three, Theodore Dreiser was born, later to become the great naturalistic Chicago novelist, a good friend of Masters, and an important influence on his *Spoon River* volume. This was the year of the great Chicago fire, the year John Hay published his *Pike County Ballads* of rural Illinois, and the year that Edward Eggleston, in *The Hoosier Schoolmaster*, an early regional novel depicting Indiana country manners in the local idiom, inaugurated a "Hoosier School" of Midwestern regionalism. Eggleston's influence eventually affected every Midwestern writer.

In the centennial year 1876, the greatest writer of the Mississippi River Valley, Mark Twain, published *Tom Sawyer*, the first of his three most important books which gave to the world the great river as archetype and symbol. The importance of *Tom Sawyer* to Masters may constitute an early "turning point"—a favorite term of Masters in his biographical writing—in the stream of events of his life and career. Between that summer of 1876, when Masters was eight, and 1878 when he and Mitch Miller drifted apart after the death of Masters's brother Alex, Lee and Mitch had a profound boyhood friendship based on Twain's book. In their relationship, as Masters gives it in *Mitch Miller* and *Skeeters Kirby*, Mitch was Tom and Lee was Huck, sharing books and adventures around Petersburg, pretending their Sangamon River was the Mississippi (which eventually, after joining the Illinois River, it indeed became).

Besides permanently imbuing Masters with river consciousness and a sense of himself in a Mississippi River orientation (if the predominance of water signs in his horoscope had not previously so inclined him), Twain became important to Masters as a model, much as Huck and Tom had been models to young Lee and Mitch. In Masters's fiction the two boys actually receive a letter signed by "Tom Sawyer" and run off together in an attempt to visit him at Hannibal, Missouri.[2] The novel *Mitch Miller*, including the first fifty pages of its sequel *Skeeters Kirby*, is in many respects modeled on *Tom Sawyer*, even to a minor point, a curious, probably unconscious, echo of Twain. In his narration of Mitch's death and the subsequent birth to Mrs. Miller of a baby boy, Masters oddly names the boy Charles William, adding that "he only lived three or four years and then died."[3] Charles William Allbright appears in the famous raftsmen passage that Twain moved from *Huckleberry Finn* to *Life on the Mississippi*. He is a double fiction, appearing in a raftsman's yarn as a murdered baby three years dead floating in a barrel and bringing bad luck to raftsmen. He is also, for a moment, one of the many pseudonyms of Huck, who had been hiding on the raft listening to the story.

Twain was a model to Masters as a father is a model whom the son emulates and resents and tries to surpass and whom he may be tempted to discredit. In *Across Spoon River* Masters mentions two such father figures as he compares his childhood home in Lewistown with Mark Twain's home in Hannibal, Missouri (which had a certain attractiveness), and Whitman's birthplace (which had comfort and even beauty). His own home in contrast seemed to him unkempt and ugly (*ASR,* 65). Besides the presumption that these three great American authors may be considered together, there is the slightly resentful tone that the other two had fewer obstacles to overcome than he. In his biography *Mark Twain*, Masters emphasizes certain parallels. After describing Twain's apprenticeship on the *Missouri Courier* at Hannibal, he talks about newspaper practice "in those days, and in my time when I was doing similar work on *The News* of Lewistown, Illinois."[4] He mentions numerous other parallels, though he does not mention them *as* parallels: that Twain also was son of a lawyer and of parents who did not love one another; that from the age of four to eleven Twain spent much of his time on a farm with beloved relatives, enjoying sumptuous country meals; that Hannibal, where he moved with his family while still an infant, was settled, like Masters's Petersburg, by people from Kentucky, Virginia, and Tennessee; that as a boy Twain was familiar with fights and killings in the streets, with drownings and terrifying lightning storms; that he became a printer's apprentice for the town newspaper; that his early literary interests were centered in reading the stories of Edgar Allan Poe; that a major event in his life came from a book he chanced upon—for Masters it was the volume of Shelley, for Twain an account of exploration of the Amazon River.[5]

In the same year that Twain published *Tom Sawyer* (1876), the telephone was invented, an event which ten years later gave Masters one of his earliest jobs in Lewistown as a part-time telephone operator. This job, in a room over a drugstore where the druggist manufactured home remedies (*ASR,* 76), was the source of much of the material of the later *Spoon River* epitaphs. In that of "Edith Bell," from *The New Spoon River* (1924), the speaker confesses that as the local telephone operator "over Trainor's drug store" she was privy to all the gossip and assignations of Spoon River. Also in 1876 Sherwood Anderson was born, much later to have his career strangely intertwined with that of Masters.

In 1878 and 1879, respectively, when Masters was about ten, Carl Sandburg and Vachel Lindsay were born, later and to this day to have their names associated with that of Edgar Lee Masters as the Chicago poets of the American poetic renaissance which began about 1912. Sandburg was a friend and perhaps a source at the time Masters was writing the Spoon River poems in 1914; later Masters came to dislike Sandburg and wrote his biography *Lincoln: The Man* partially to correct Sandburg's laudatory portrait of Lincoln. Lindsay he also knew as a friend around 1912, as Lindsay's mother and Emma Masters were at this time close friends in Springfield, Illinois; Masters's later biography *Vachel Lindsay* (1935), written after Lindsay's suicide, is cordial and sympathetic.

In 1879 Henry George published *Progress and Poverty*, condemning monopoly in land ownership and proposing his solution of the Single Tax on land. It was part of a general reformist wave that produced the protest journalism of the muckrakers, most notably Upton Sinclair's story of the Chicago stockyards, *The Jungle* (1906), and the Populist Movement of the Midwest that culminated in the defeat of William Jennings Bryan for the presidency in 1896. Masters, an ardent champion of Bryan at the time (he long treasured a silver dollar given him by Bryan), later castigated Twain for his failure to read or understand Henry George's book and for his failure as a social critic. Certainly Henry George supported Masters's own Jeffersonian agrarianism. Perhaps Masters's Lewistown girl friend Margaret George became, in *Skeeters Kirby*, "Winifred Henry" in indirect tribute to Henry George. The *Spoon River* epitaph "George Trimble" includes both Henry George and Bryan, "the Peerless Leader."

About 1882 Masters, at the age of fourteen, began writing verses. In that year James Whitcomb Riley published his book of sentimental Hoosier lyrics *The Ole Swimmin' Hole*; in 1883 Eugene Field began his "Sharps and Flats" column in the *Chicago Daily News*; and by 1888 Lee and his friend Margaret were contributing spoofs of Riley to Field's column.

In the 1880s Midwestern novelists were beginning to look with critical, realistic eyes at Midwestern farm life and the country town. In 1883 E. W. Howe published *The Story of a Country Town*, a pessimistic story of interrelated lives and sexual complications and frustrations, a naturalistic novel written nearly twenty years before Dreiser's *Sister Carrie* (1900), thirty years before *Spoon River*. In 1885 Twain published *Huckleberry Finn*, in which the descriptions of life along the Mississippi shores approximate Masters's later view of Lewistown along the Spoon, while the descriptions of Huck and Jim's idyllic life on the raft parallel Masters's memories of Petersburg and his grandparents' farm. In the 1880s Hamlin Garland was writing his tales of the life journey of the poor and the weary along the *Main Travelled Roads* (1891) of the Middle West—those who unlike Masters's travelers had not yet completed their journeys. In 1887 Joseph Kirkland's realistic novel of the Midwest, *Zury*, presented a plot resembling that of the *Spoon River* portrait "Else Wertman," in which to cover an adultery a child is suffered to grow up without knowing his true parent, who lives in the same town unable to express her natural affection.

In the economic-political arena during this period, the Haymarket Riot occurred in Chicago in May 1886, two weeks before Masters graduated from the Lewistown high school. In 1888 Edward Bellamy's response to the Haymarket upheaval was the utopian novel *Looking Backward*; its great popularity fomented political optimism and the belief that existing evils such as slums and social and economic inequalities were remediable. Like Henry George's *Progress and Poverty* it encouraged enthusiastic reformist politics. If Masters failed to see Bellamy's book in these years, it was called to his attention later during his partnership after 1903 with Clarence Darrow, who was president of the Bellamy Club in Chicago. Bellamy's vision, however, failed to appeal for long to Masters for several reasons. Bellamy was in the line of New England reformers, while Masters considered himself a Southern philosopher. Bellamy's program was a technology organized for production in a regimented state, while Masters, essentially a Jeffersonian agrarian, opposed both technology and political centralization; Bellamy's vision was prospective, with emphasis on the state; Masters's was retrospective, with emphasis on the individual.

Three *R*'s and the End of Education

The contrast between Masters's later views and the views of Bellamy illustrates three related yet opposing tendencies—romanticism, realism, and reformism—which characterize the thought and literature of the period. All three affected Masters directly while he was coming of age and absorbing the ideas in the world about him. First, he was affected by the romanticism of the frontier, the sentimental appreciation of the old free ways—of the South before the Civil War, the homestead before the town, the village before the city. Second, he responded to the realistic appraisal of the environment—farm, village, city—and its frank admission of social and human limitations, pessimistic, approaching the naturalistic view of Dreiser, for instance, that men and women are but pawns moved here and there by biological and environmental forces beyond their control. Third, Masters was affected by reformism, which admitted the evils but was optimistically determined to correct them. All three entered his thinking and writing and can be observed in specific epitaphs or portraits of the *Spoon River Anthology*.

Romanticism is evident in the ancestral portraits, "Lucinda Matlock" and "Rebecca Wasson," pioneers who lived in the good old time, and in the epitaph of the country musician "Fiddler Jones." Realism can be seen in the initial *Spoon River* portrait, "Hod Putt" ("hard put"?), a man who interpreted the bankruptcy laws in his own way by robbing and killing a stranger, and in the forthright descriptions of the petty lives, the crimes, the lusts, the deaths among other citizens of Spoon River. The reformist tendency is implicit in the pictures of the villains, "A. D. Blood," mayor and industrialist, "Thomas Rhodes," president of the bank, "Editor Whedon" of the *Spoon River Argus*, "The Circuit Judge," and others who oppressed and judged the poor and the weak and innocent; and it is explicit in the didacticisms of many epitaphs: "Robert Southey Burke" warns against believing in ideals or giving love to a man; "Mrs. Charles Bliss" cries out disdainfully against judges and preachers; "John Hancock Otis" warns against those who rise to power from rural poverty.

By the early 1890s the Midwest had attained a self-conscious identity distinct from the East, the South, the Far West. It had developed its own Midwest regional literature. Gradually this Midwest consciousness was centering in Chicago—from the Ohio and Indiana of William Dean Howells and Eggleston and the Hoosier school, from the upper Midwest of Hamlin Garland, from Twain's Hannibal, Missouri. Masters, though conscious of the New England and Southern elements in his background, was not yet a conscious Midwesterner. He still needed the perspective which he could attain by distance, by time, or by familiarity with a contrasting environment from which to view Lewistown and Petersburg. That perspective was to be provided by Chicago.

Chapter Three

Chicago: The Way to Spoon River

"The Most Glorious Summer"

The significance of Chicago to Masters was complex. At first it was simply the big city, the economic and political center, the source and destination of goods, services, money, people. Then it became opportunity, excitement, escape from parental domination. After Masters came to live there in July 1892, the city acquired still other meanings.

When the *Spoon River Anthology* appeared in 1914–15, Masters had lived one quarter of his life in the Petersburg area, one quarter in Lewistown, one half in Chicago. Masters recognizes roughly this proportion in devoting two thirds of *Across Spoon River* to his Chicago years. Chicago, he says, brought him face to face with reality and an active life and cured him of "the pathos" of rural life (*ASR,* 404). Once again he stresses in relation to a particular place certain persons and events that influenced his life. The central persons, all directing him toward his major achievement, were—with the continuing influence of his grandmother and his mother—Ernest McGaffey, an early friend in Chicago; Clarence Darrow; Tennessee Mitchell, a lover; Theodore Dreiser; William Marion Reedy, editor of the St. Louis weekly *Mirror*; and the poet Carl Sandburg. The major events were the Chicago World's Fair or Columbian Exposition in the summer of 1893—which Masters called "the most glorious" summer of his life (*ASR,* 171); the great love affair of his Chicago years, with Tennessee Mitchell from 1909 to 1911; and the writing and publishing of the "Spoon River" poems in 1914, "the really glorious year" (*ASR,* 338).

Masters's objective was to find newspaper work on the *Chicago Inter-Ocean,* whose editor had published a number of his verses and otherwise encouraged him. He had already had newspaper experience on the *Lewistown News*, from setting type to writing editorials, and so arrived at the Chicago offices of the *Inter-Ocean* full of hope. The editor received him cordially, but refused to hire him into what he called the slavery of newspaper work. Then he paused, gave his visitor the address of a young man he had kept out of journalism and sent into law practice, saying if the young man did not agree he was right, Masters could have the job after all (*ASR,* 144).

A few weeks later, a very discouraged Masters found McGaffey— or Maltravers, the Dickensian name[1] by which Masters refers to him in *Across Spoon River*—after fruitless days of job-hunting and living penniless with his uncle. McGaffey was a practicing lawyer and a publishing poet who knew Masters's name because their verses had been printed together on the same Sunday page of the *Chicago Chronicle*. McGaffey welcomed Edgar Lee warmly and agreed with the editor that law was a better occupation for a poet than newspaper work, which would harm one's style. McGaffey became Masters's friend in need and served him as a companion and guide to some of the complexities of Chicago life. He took Masters to the Press Club and introduced him to Opie Read and John McGovern and other literary figures of the Chicago scene who frequented the Press Club.

Masters's first job in Chicago, except for a one-day stint setting type, was as a bill collector for the Edison Company, a job which he abhorred. Evenings at the Press Club provided a certain amount of relief from this job. Its members were a bawdy group of mostly rural men who had emigrated to Chicago. The men of the Press Club were easy for Masters to identify with, doubtless because they offered him a better status than he might have hoped for elsewhere in more intellectual literary clubs. Masters describes his companions as mostly "habitually broke," hearty drinkers who composed lewd verses to entertain each other.[2] Opie Read recounts some bawdy adventures at the Press Club during the World's Fair, including Egyptian dancing girls who danced naked at the club, "their faces in dark seclusion, but all else exposed to the glaring light." He recalls, "they would stand to be caressed, fondled in giggling fun, but shuddered back in Mohammedan repulsion if wine were offered."[3]

This friendly male companionship and the release of rural repressions through the writing of pornographic verse were important to Masters, especially during his first uneasy years in Chicago, without

connections or associates. Habit or nostalgia for these early Press
Club years must have contributed to his lifelong custom of writing
pornographic verses and comments in letters to intimate friends of
both sexes, in half-serious poems, and mostly in a tremendous store
of unpublished miscellany written mainly under a variety of pseudonyms like "Lute [or "Lewd"] Puckett," "Elmer Chubb," "Dr.
Atherton." One of these, "To a Spirochaeta," he unfortunately published in *The Great Valley* (1916); another, a lyric entitled "Fellatio,"
though more effective may never know print.

In 1893, just before the Fair opened, McGaffey introduced Masters to a former law associate of his with the "astonishing name"—
never mentioned in the autobiography—Kicksham Scanlon (*ASR*,
167). He and Masters immediately formed a law association, Scanlon
insisting that Masters use his full name Edgar Lee Masters. On the
first of May, the same day that the Columbian Exposition opened,
they opened their new office. It was only ten months since Masters
had arrived in Chicago—the glorious summer was beginning (*ASR*,
167–68).

The effect of the Fair on Masters, as on most thoughtful persons
who attended, including its most noted literary commentator, Henry
Adams, was symbolic. To Adams, fascinated by modern power, the
dynamos on exhibit became symbols of infinity. "Chicago asked in
1893 for the first time the question whether the American people
knew where they were driving" or being driven by the forces about
them. "Chicago [the fair] was the first expression of American thought
as a unity; one must start there."[4] For Masters, thirty years Adams's
junior, the fair was fascinating in more immediate and practical
ways. He enjoyed the night life with his new associate Scanlon and
their dates, and on free days he frequented the art exhibits, making
notes for poems. But Masters was as aware as Adams of Chicago as
a force, asserting itself by centripetal pull—a unifying center. Chicago, Masters recounts, was full of people who had flocked from
throughout the Midwest to make money from the fair (*ASR*, 183).
The elderly Adams saw the inevitable drift of forces to a capitalistic
economy and resigned himself to it. Masters felt it and fought it
for the rest of his life.

Nevertheless, Chicago in 1893 gave Masters the heady sense of
being at the center of things, of being able to look out from the
still point at the hub and watch the movement of people and events
and at the same time to feel himself a part of that movement. In

his association with Scanlon he found a new security and sense of independence and progress in the legal profession. In his friendship with McGaffey and with members of the Press Club, he could enjoy a new leisure and feel an identity with others: Midwesterners from farms and small towns, drawn like himself into the urban whorl of Chicago, the center of the new world. Combined with his visits to his home territory in the Spoon and Sangamon country—especially visits he made the year after the fair, with McGaffey—Chicago and the fair gave Masters at once a sense of separateness and a sense of unity. His sense of separateness from his village background allowed him the perspective to see his background with realistic eyes. His sense of unity, of oneness with other Midwesterners like himself, of being at the center of events, gave him a perception of the identity of human lives whether in the village microcosm or the urban macrocosm. It supported his natural optimism of energy and youth, his inherited Jeffersonianism, his belief (corroborated by reading in Herberet Spencer of the doctrine of inevitable progress) in the perfectibility of man.

Perspectives on Spoon River

From his vantage point in Chicago, Masters made frequent visits to Lewistown and Petersburg, the most important of them in 1894, in 1906, and again in 1909, just before his grandmother's death in January 1910. In the summer of 1894 McGaffey accompanied him as he visited Lewistown and his grandparents' farm. McGaffey became friendly with the citizens of Lewistown, visited, according to Masters, the "landmarks" of Masters's childhood in the Petersburg area, and familiarized himself with all of Masters's background (*ASR*, 179–80). In effect McGaffey recaptured Masters's past, saw it through Masters's eyes, and gave Masters the opportunity to see it through his. From this time forward, Masters had a perspective on the people, the places, the events of his youth which he never lost. His perspective only broadened as he learned of new events and saw the familiar through others' eyes, one of whom was Darr, who had taught him logic and Latin in Lewistown and was now practicing law in Chicago; for a time they saw much of one another and would debate the contrasts between city and country (*ASR*, 186). Others included Masters's father, who occasionally visited him in Chicago; his mother; and his sister Madeline Stone, who had married into

wealthy Chicago society during Masters's first year in Chicago, and
who in fact, Masters mentions, was visiting Lewistown with her
husband and daughter during his visit with McGaffey.

Before McGaffey went with Masters to Lewistown, he found other
ways to be of use to him in his literary ambitions. It was McGaffey
who found Masters his first publishers, Way & Williams, the firm
which contracted to publish his *A Book of Verses* but went bankrupt
just before the book was to appear in 1898. McGaffey also promoted
Maximilian, Masters's early poetic drama, and found it a Boston
publisher, Richard G. Badger, who issued it in 1902. McGaffey's
most valuable service was to introduce Masters to William Marion
Reedy. McGaffey was an old friend of the St. Louis editor, whom
he recognized as a generous man who made a practice of publishing
unknown but promising writers. When Reedy published McGaffey's
verses in his weekly *Mirror*, McGaffey thought he should publish
as well those of Masters. McGaffey sent Reedy more than one sheaf
of Masters's verses, sometimes with a laudatory review attached.
Reedy was unimpressed with Masters as a poet, but finally met him
about 1907 when Masters came to St. Louis on law business with
a letter from McGaffey. They became acquaintances, corresponded
frequently, and ultimately became fast friends. It was Reedy who
first published the *Spoon River Anthology* serially in his *Mirror* in
1914.

In short, McGaffey did everything he could, as a friend and
admirer of Masters, and as an established resident of Chicago, to
introduce him to the city, to prod him toward poetry and a circle
of people among whom poetry was appreciated. As Reedy put it,
"McGaffey's real contribution was to recognize Masters' poetic talent
at a stage when it would have been imperceptible to anyone who
did not love him as a friend."[5]

It should be noted that Reedy's disparagement of Masters's early
work was the comment of another friend—as well as a judicious
literary critic and admirer—of Masters. Before Reedy accepted the
first Spoon River poems for the *Mirror*, Masters had written eight
or more plays and three volumes of verse, and had published two
works of nonfiction. The drama was written not so much for itself
as in the hope of making money—enough so that Masters could
retire from law practice and devote himself to literature. The verse
is typical, fairly competent newspaper verse of the time—nothing

more. The nonfiction is political and reformist, of the nature of tracts.

This nonfiction prose which Masters was writing at the turn of the century was influenced by his political activities in behalf of Bryan and the Democratic party in the election of 1896 and afterward to about 1908. Masters was especially determined to combat the tendency toward imperialism of turn-of-the-century America, and engaged in extensive studies and writing in his anti-imperialist patriotic fervor (*ASR*, 404–5). He published essays in the *Jeffersonian Magazine* and in the *Chicago Chronicle* and later collected them as *The New Star Chamber* (1904). They undoubtedly influenced his law practice, as he became more and more the intercessor and less and less attractive to the wealthy and the corporations.

In 1896 Masters—whose father, a delegate, gave him a ticket—attended the Democratic convention in Chicago and heard Bryan's famous Cross of Gold speech. Masters was inspired by the possibilities of Populism. During the 1896 election, he devoted his enormous energy to the campaign, writing articles and essays and giving a speech on free silver in Petersburg. He worked for twenty-two hours at the election polls. And he was bitterly disappointed at Bryan's defeat.

1896 was a pivotal year in other respects. In this year, perhaps while he was in Petersburg for the free-silver speech, Masters visited his grandparents at the farm, where he quizzed his grandmother and had her swear out an affidavit as to her family, in a lawyerlike desire to get all the facts down on paper (*ASR*, 6). It was on this occasion that he learned, with evident pleasure, that she was an illegitimate child or "love-child" (*ASR*, 7). In the literary world, relevant events of 1896 were Edwin Arlington Robinson's publication of his first Tilbury Town portraits in *The Torrent and the Night Before* and in England A. E. Housman's *A Shropshire Lad*, both picturing the macrocosm through the rural or village microcosm, as Masters was to do in the *Spoon River Anthology*. In England again, Thomas Hardy turned from naturalistic novelist to lyric poet of the "Wessex" microcosm. In America, the success of Stephen Crane's *Red Badge of Courage* (1895) made possible the republication of *Maggie* (1893, 1896), a novel notable, in the words of literary historian Robert E. Spiller, for "its unprecedented candor of theme, its sense of fate, and its directness in dealing with sordid material. . . . With that [publication] modern American fiction was born.''[6] The identical words, substituting "poetry" for "fiction," might be applied to Masters's *Spoon River Anthology*, which appeared just twenty years later.

In 1898 Masters's *Book of Verses* was printed, though never published because of the bankruptcy of the publishers. In that year Masters made another of his frequent trips to Lewistown, only fifty miles from Chicago, this time with his partner, Scanlon. They visited the cemetery there and as they stood beside a Revolutionary soldier's grave suddenly they heard the various church bells of the town begin to ring (*ASR,* 237–38). The Spanish-American War had been declared, the source of Masters's fervor against American "imperialism" and of the *Chronicle* articles that became *The New Star Chamber*. This particular occasion was also the source of the *Spoon River* poem "John Wasson," in which a Revolutionary soldier— Masters's great-great-grandfather—speaks ironically of a soldier "who fought the Filipinos."

Also in 1898 Masters married Helen Jenkins, attracted to her by her beauty and by his loneliness, and by his need for someone to do his sewing and to take care of his laundry. But a "controlling" factor, he says, in his decision to marry after earlier convincing himself that he would never do so, was the problem of sex. He wished to end the painful series of love affairs in devotion to a wife to whom in exchange he was willing to promise absolute "fidelity" (*ASR,* 230). Another attraction was her father's status in Chicago. Masters believed that his wife's father, a railroad president, would offer him a salaried position, and he would at last have leisure to write (*ASR,* 230). No doubt his sewing and laundry were taken care of, but his marriage failed to solve the problem of sex (after various infidelities he was divorced in 1923), the job with the railroad never materialized, and he attained leisure to write only *after* his best work, *Spoon River*, was published.

Also in 1898, however, Masters had occasion to get a "famous criminal lawyer" in Chicago appointed as attorney for the receiver of a bankrupt company (*ASR,* 270). This lawyer then, and again in 1903, when he was reorganizing the law firm of John Peter Altgeld (the ex-governor whom Masters knew and admired), invited Masters to join his firm. On the second occasion, having come to a disagreeable break with his associate, Scanlon, Masters accepted. In his autobiography, Masters scrupulously avoids, as with Scanlon, any mention of the name of this lawyer with whom he maintained an office for seven years in the Ashland Block in Chicago; yet he includes in *Across Spoon River* many details about his partner's character and describes with bitterness the events which led to the dissolution of their partnership in 1911.

This unnamed "famous criminal lawyer" was Clarence Darrow, who is still remembered as the lawyer who unsuccessfully debated the fundamentalist views of William Jennings Bryan in the Scopes Trial, the "Monkey Trial" of 1925. Darrow had come to Chicago in 1888, four years before Masters. Here, according to his own autobiography *The Story of My Life* (1932), he "discovered a little book . . . [which] was to make its author my idol, and my life what it is."[7] The little book was Altgeld's *Our Penal Code and Its Victims* (1884) in which Altgeld presented his philosophy of crime and his humanitarian legal theories. In 1894 Darrow resigned as a prosperous railway lawyer to devote himself to labor and political cases in the spirit of Altgeld.

Masters, like Darrow, idolized Altgeld. They had other things in common. Both had been born in small Midwestern towns, then moved to Chicago. More interestingly, both had already tried their hands at literature, and both had published two books by the time they became partners in 1903. The following year, 1904, Masters published his *New Star Chamber* and Darrow published at his own expense his only novel, *Farmington*.

Farmington was Darrow's fictional name for the small town which was his childhood home. The story is a reminiscence in which the narrator tells of revisiting his home town as an adult. "Last summer I went back to linger, like a ghost, around the old familiar spot." In chapter 1 the narrator apologizes for taking "the reader to my grave in the very first chapter of the book." At the end, he remembers that "when I asked for familiar names, over and over again I was pointed to the white stones that now covered our old playground and were persistently crawling up the hill. . . ."[8] The novel, like the later *Spoon River Anthology*, is a recounting of the small-town lives of remembered characters who have died, and their hopes and failures.

In 1906, before sailing to Europe with his wife, Masters returned to Petersburg to visit his grandmother, then ninety years old. At this time, he tells us in *Across Spoon River*, he spoke with his father of his projected "only book," which was to be a novel based upon his childhood home and acquaintances. This concept, he says, was the "germ" of his famous *Anthology* (*ASR*, 286).

It was a germ that closely resembled *Farmington*, which may have been the germ of the germ, though we do not know with certainty that Masters read Darrow's novel. Actually the relationship between the two men remains somewhat mysterious. After the dissolution of their partnership, their relations became increasingly strained; Darrow served as lawyer for Mrs. Masters in their divorce action in 1923. In the early thirties both men wrote their autobiographies; neither mentioned the name of the other. Darrow does appear, however, in some of Masters's fiction, notably as Cavette Errant in the novel *Mirage* (1924) and as David Barrow in *Domesday Book* and especially in its sequel *The Fate of the Jury*.

The point to be made here about the two lawyer-writers—as about Masters, Edwin Arlington Robinson, Sherwood Anderson, and William Faulkner—is not the indebtedness of one to another: it is their common re-creation of their small-town environments. Their portraits of their towns and townspeople, drawn with differing mixtures of affection and distaste, emerged in part out of the psychological necessities of their time. The rapid urbanization of the period had created cities with a centripetal energy which drew to them the talented, the imaginative, the ambitious. In responding, the artists uprooted themselves to join millions of others, only less talented, who were experiencing the profound shock of removal from the stability of the micro-cosmic town to the exhilaration, the confusion, the anarchy of the rapidly expanding city. This urbanizing process occurred first in the East (Tilbury Town) of E. A. Robinson, then in the Midwest (Spoon River; Winesburg, Ohio) of Masters, Anderson, and others, then in the South (Yoknapatawpha County) of William Faulkner. In the need to bridge the chasm between the two cultures, one essentially rural and the other wholly metropolitan, there was an instinctive reaching back to the earlier one, a comparison of places, persons, and values in the search for familiar, recognizable elements on which to base judgments in the hectic new environment. Though many of the Midwestern writers who "revolted" from the village considered themselves and are generally thought of as radicals—Darrow, Masters, Anderson, Sinclair Lewis—this retrospective gesture was psychologically reactionary.

Seeds of *Spoon River:*
The *Greek Anthology* and the Nymph Calypso

Masters's close association with Ernest McGaffey lasted until McGaffey suddenly moved to the Far West in 1912, though it naturally diminished somewhat after Masters's marriage in 1898 and during his partnership with Darrow from 1903 to 1911. It was midway through this partnership, about 1907, that Masters met Reedy, through McGaffey. In 1909 Reedy called Masters's attention to, perhaps gave him a copy of, the *Greek Anthology*, a collection of ironic first-person epitaphs spoken by the dead, written in epigrammatic verse by anonymous ancient Greek writers. It is a prototype of the *Spoon River Anthology*. Masters barely mentions the *Greek Anthology* in *Across Spoon River*—in a passage explaining why he found no novelty in the free verse of Carl Sandburg (*ASR,* 336). But in his introduction, or dedication, to *Toward the Gulf* (1918), "To William Marion Reedy," he is quite explicit. Reedy, in June 1909, he says, called the *Greek Anthology* to his attention, as a result of which he "unconsciously" began the Spoon River epitaphs (vii).

There is no firm evidence that Masters immediately looked into the *Greek Anthology* in June 1909, although he says in his article "The Genesis of Spoon River" that he "read the Greek Anthology about 1909" (48). But that he probably acquired it then is indicated by the fact that he inscribed that date on the flyleaf of his copy, in which marginalia in his hand also indicate that he worked closely with that copy in composing sketches for the *Spoon River Anthology*.[9] Just when he made his marginal comments is difficult to ascertain. Probably most are from early 1914. Masters used John William Mackail's *Anthologia Graeca: Select Epigrams from the Greek Anthology* (1906).

If the "germ" of *Spoon River Anthology* was Masters's conversation with his father in 1906 about a prospective novel, perhaps related to Darrow's novel *Farmington*, the first true seeds were planted in 1909. In June Masters acquired the *Greek Anthology*; in August he began the most intense love affair of his life; in the fall he paid his final visit to his grandmother, for him the central figure of his "Spoon River" country. At the height of his love affair he asked his wife to release him (which she refused to do) so that he might marry Tennessee Mitchell, who had been piano instructor to his nieces.

From 1909 to 1911, Masters was engaged in a tumultuous love affair with Mitchell. The dates are Masters's, the subtitle to his "Ballade of Ultimate Shame: T.M., August 20, 1909–May 23, 1911," published under the pseudonym Webster Ford in *Songs and Sonnets, Second Series* (1912).

Masters returned to this central relationship in his literary career again and again in individual poems, novels, and plays, and most explicitly in the autobiography *Across Spoon River*, where he quaintly indexes under his own name some sixteen "love affairs" (the index is incomplete here and elsewhere), with "Deirdre"—that is, Tennessee Mitchell—inconspicuously listed in alphabetical order: "Deirdre, 295–314." There is no question that Tennessee Claflin Mitchell, or "T.M." in the "Ballade" mentioned above, is Deirdre. In the chapter he devotes to her in *Across Spoon River*, Masters mentions "the Claflin sisters" (she was named for the feminist Tennessee Claflin) as well as accurate details of her early life. In a letter of 25 May 1941 Masters dictated to the second Mrs. Masters a response to a researcher, William L. Phillips, asserting that Mitchell was indeed the Deirdre of *Across Spoon River*. More recently Mrs. Masters has said of her, "Tennessee Mitchell was a very intelligent and courageous woman—a real person."[10] In the Tennessee chapter one finds, as often in Masters, considerable bitterness that people and events failed to work out as they might have. Yet in commenting on one of Tennessee's final letters he says his doubts of her may have been the product of his own jealousies (*ASR,* 309). Then he says it took him "three years" to "extirpate" Tennessee's venom from his system and that one never fully recovers from such an experience, though it can be rigorously instructive mentally and emotionally. Tennessee, he asserts, taught him the joys and sorrows of lovers of all times and greatly deepened his "emotional powers" (312–13). Writing a quarter of a century after the events, he remains so convinced of her effect on his powers of insight and sympathy as an artist that he insists that he would have been unable to write a number of his poems without her rigorous instruction (*ASR,* 313). He could not in fact have written *Spoon River Anthology.*

This crucial episode is intimately tied, in his autobiography and in his psyche, to Masters's last visit to his grandmother, who died the following January. In the midst of his love affair he sought solace in the fall of 1909 from his grandmother, who had reached her ninety-sixth year. In the rural Petersburg which he had loved as a child, his grandmother talked about the local people now recognizable as *Spoon River* portraits, even mentioning Masters's great-great-grandmother, Rebecca Wasson (*ASR*, 302–4). As she talked on, Masters confesses, he "was thinking of [Tennessee]" (*ASR*, 304). So the stories of Petersburg and later, by association, of nearby Lewistown came to Masters in his state of emotional hypersensitivity, conscious that he was looking his last at his beloved grandmother (*ASR*, 304) and that he could never reconcile his love for Tennessee with his marriage, his children, his career as a lawyer. With his mind in Chicago, doubtless he scarcely heard his grandmother's words but absorbed the pictures and characters directly into his memories of what was to become the composite village Spoon River.

It took "three years" from the end of the affair on "May 23, 1911" for Masters to "extirpate" Tennessee's venom. All art, whatever else it may be, is catharsis. As he had sought solace in traveling to Petersburg in 1909, so he found relief in 1914 in the imaginative journey to Spoon River. In May 1914, three years to the month, the first of his Spoon River epitaphs appeared in *Reedy's Mirror*. In August, the fifth anniversary of the beginning of the affair, appeared the epitaph "Tennessee Claflin Shope"—spoken by a voice of indeterminate sex who has found peace. Ten years after their parting, Masters celebrated Tennessee as the nymph Calypso in the poem "Ulysses" from *The Open Sea* (1921). Speaking as Ulysses, he asks, "What's a woman?" and answers, "She is . . . the Muse." Tennessee was, after all, his "good daemon."

Chapter Four
Widening Horizons: Literary Friends and Influences

In telling of the conclusion of the Tennessee Mitchell affair in *Across Spoon River,* Masters says, with what seems a sigh in which are mingled relief and regret, that "the end" had come, followed by a "long convalescence" (*ASR,* 312). The three years of convalescence (May 1911 to May 1914) coincided with the latter part of a five-year gestation period in which the seeds sown in Masters's mind in 1909 could grow to maturity. During that time three literary men— Dreiser the novelist, Carl Sandburg the poet, and Reedy the editor— influenced their growth.

Theodore Dreiser

When Ernest McGaffey came to Chicago in 1912 to say goodbye to Masters, Masters says he was "stunned" (*ASR,* 284), though he had seen but little of McGaffey in the past three years. Not many days later, he says in the following paragraph, he was reading Dreiser's *Sister Carrie* (1900), just republished after twelve years' suppression by "Comstockery." He wrote a letter congratulating Dreiser, who replied soon afterward, and their acquaintance was begun. Masters's brother-the-god, seemingly acting in the person of McGaffey, had encouraged Masters's literary aspirations, had introduced him to others who could help him, and had found him publishers. Now the fraternal deity seemed suddenly to be transmogrified into Dreiser, his latest avatar—except that Reedy was continuing in a very similar role.

Almost immediately Masters and Dreiser exchanged letters of introduction; Masters sent Dreiser an introduction to Judge Carter Harrison, who could help Dreiser with information on the Chicago industrialist Charles T. Yerkes, the subject of *The Financier* and of *The Titan* (1914) then in progress. Dreiser sent Masters an intro-

34

duction to the critic and editor of the *Smart Set,* H. L. Mencken, whom Masters was anxious to meet and whom he later considered a good friend. Once the Spoon River epitaphs began to appear, Dreiser also wrote to Mencken, commending to his attention the Chicago literary scene in general and Masters in particular.

Early in 1913 Dreiser went to Chicago in order to gather material on Yerkes for *The Titan.* He visited Masters to get names of lawyers, editors, and businessmen who had known Yerkes. Masters recalls the visit in *Across Spoon River,* and says that he saw much of Dreiser while he was in Chicago. On one occasion during a walk together, Dreiser told Masters the plot of a forthcoming novel (*The Bulwark,* 1946), which sounded as though Dreiser had known Masters's father-in-law, the railroad executive. Such conversations and exchanges were frequent between Masters and Dreiser. Most of their encounters were by mail, but some took place in person, especially when Masters moved to New York about 1920.

They discussed matters of politics, literature, and philosophy in their letters and conversations; they discussed each other's work both prospective and completed; they sent each other proofs to read and advised and criticized each other. For two years they wrote each other regularly.

About February or March 1914, Dreiser was back in Chicago, and Masters took him along to central Illinois to visit the Petersburg area. They stayed in Oakford, about ten miles from Petersburg, at the home of John Armstrong, a local fiddler and a long-time friend of Masters's father. Here the two writers were entertained with stories and anecdotes of local folk, and with hearty food prepared by Mrs. Armstrong. Dreiser, at least indirectly, had been encouraging Masters around this time to turn toward his Illinois experience for poetic material. Masters had written to him in September 1913 that he could give Dreiser ample material for stories of Illinois, though nothing more than character portrayals of real people. Did Masters realize at the time of the visit to Oakford that character portrayals of real people were exactly the kind of material which would prove so rich in *Spoon River Anthology* only months later? Certainly he realized he had something.

Much later he recounted in *The Sangamon* the Oakford visit to John Armstrong. Armstrong "was re-creating the atmosphere of the past for me," and Masters was "steering" the conversation so that he could get "that village [New Salem] and its people on the Sangamon into my imagination." Following the talk, Masters and Dreiser visited the Oakford Cemetery, where Masters wanted "to note the names of people" he remembered from his boyhood days on his grandfather's farm (97, 102, 108).

Of course Masters is writing thirty years after the event, but he clearly gives the impression that on this visit with Dreiser in early 1914 he was collecting names and memories from his past for some use. However, the instigator of the visit, Masters says in *The Sangamon*, was Dreiser. Masters had never met John Armstrong but had heard much about him from his father, and he regaled Dreiser with these stories when Dreiser came to Chicago to collect material for his novel. Dreiser "became anxious at once to go to Oakford. He wanted to meet him, and down we went . . . ." (93).

Related to his realism in *Sister Carrie* and later novels was Dreiser's irony, his naturalistic sense of fate controlling human lives, as well as his somewhat contradictory meliorism, by which he hoped to better the human condition by exposing social evils like sexual repression and political evils like capitalism. In 1912 Masters had read Dreiser with admiration for his revelation of the facts of life in America and for his open discussion of sexual relationships. Here was precedent and encouragement for Masters too to deal directly and honestly with "the facts of life." Masters had already published strongly stated political exposés. That he first published the sexual exposés of his *Spoon River Anthology* under a pseudonym was certainly an attempt to protect his law practice, his livelihood—protect them not so much from the Comstocks as from prospective clients who subscribed to the prevalent notion that poets are effete and impractical and not to be trusted in practical affairs.

By late March 1914 Masters had been rereading the *Greek Anthology* and had begun jotting down his own "anthologies," one or more each Sunday, as he notes in "The Genesis of Spoon River" (49). He had begun a work pattern, though he had not yet consciously begun "Spoon River Anthology." He was nearing the end of an enervating legal battle on behalf of striking waitresses. Drama, rather than poetry, seemed to him the appropriate genre for exploiting his Illinois background, as Dreiser had urged him to do. On 29 May the first of his Spoon River poems appeared in *Reedy's Mirror* (the name changed from the *Mirror* to *Reedy's Mirror* in 1913, after Reedy assumed ownership), and by October Reedy had sent to Dreiser the complete files to date of the *Mirror* containing the

Spoon River poems, which Dreiser used in seeking a publisher. On 19 March 1915, a publisher, Macmillan, having been found, Masters sent the proof sheets to Dreiser to show to John Cowper Powys, whose lectures and articles were to do much to make Masters and his *Spoon River Anthology* famous.

The friendship that began in 1912 lasted—except for a rupture in the twenties—until Dreiser's death in 1945. During the rupture H. L. Mencken wrote to Dreiser suggesting a rendezvous for the three of them. Dreiser held back: "I'm a little off Edgar Lee. Ask me not. . . . It was I who persuaded him to crystallize his little broodings into the *Spoon River Anthology*. He sent most of them to me and I took them to Lane [Dreiser's publishers] who rejected them. Reedy began to publish them after they were sent to me."[1] This is very close to the truth. Evidently "Theodore the Poet," based on Dreiser's visit to the Sangamon, and other portraits were sent to Dreiser before they appeared in print. And Dreiser did take them to his publisher, though after most of them had already appeared.

This evidence of Dreiser's friendly encouragement and guidance shows him helping Masters to bring his experiences and sources into focus. It needed only a touch on the focusing mirror by Sandburg to brighten the image, and the sure hand of Reedy to adjust the lens so that Masters saw clearly what lay under his eye.

Carl Sandburg

According to Max Putzel in his biography of Reedy, Masters met Carl Sandburg "just before Christmas in 1913."[2] Their acquaintance began at a particularly opportune time, at the start of "the really glorious year," 1914 (*ASR*, 338). Masters was on the verge of creating *Spoon River Anthology,* and the period was one of incredible stimulation. He had nearly recovered from the traumatic love affair with Tennessee Mitchell; he had become solidly acquainted with Reedy, and had become fast friends with Dreiser; the *Greek Anthology* was stirring his imagination as had his Oakford visit with Dreiser. Now he met Sandburg and began exchanging poetic ruminations with him.

During this winter of 1913–14, when Masters was at work as attorney for the union in the important waitresses' strike, Sandburg was reporting for a newspaper called the *Day Book,* and he came to interview the union lawyer, thus initiating their acquaintance. Masters recounts that Sandburg showed him several short "prose poems" he had written, which Masters found interesting, asserting that Sandburg was breaking through on a "new trail" (*ASR*, 335–36). This seems like generous implicit recognition of a debt to Sandburg, since the two poets followed in many respects, at least at that time, the same trail blazed with the tenets of imagism and free verse. But in the same paragraph, Masters denies the debt with a remark that he saw no novelty in Sandburg's work, except in his prose.

That spring and the following fall Sandburg saw the "Spoon River" poems being written, in between court sessions, on napkins and the backs of envelopes. The two poets became close friends. Sandburg would call on Masters frequently to see his latest poems, which he praised enthusiastically (*ASR*, 339), Sandburg in turn would show his poems to Masters, who showed his appreciation of their "rude realism" (*ASR*, 340). Masters admits that he might have read Sandburg's poem, "Chicago," at this time, and it is likely that he did see it in the March 1914 issue of *Poetry* or as reprinted by Reedy. But then he goes on to say that he found it extravagant and that clearly Sandburg did not know the real Chicago of the middle class that Masters knew (*ASR*, 337).

But Sandburg knew another Chicago, which Masters had not known. As they went about together, Masters became aware of a new Chicago of artists and writers, of both sexes living freely together "just as . . . in Paris." It was a "miraculous" year (*ASR*, 340). So Sandburg introduced Masters to the flourishing artistic bohemia in Chicago. He also served as a link between Masters and *Poetry* magazine, founded by Harriet Monroe in 1912. Masters had known of the magazine and had purchased copies (*ASR*, 337), which may account for the imagistic quality of his "Spoon River" poems, since Ezra Pound, the first impresario of imagism, was publishing his imagist strictures there frequently (including "A Few Don'ts for an Imagist" in March 1913). But Edgar Lee Masters was still unknown to *Poetry*. According to Monroe in her autobiography, *A Poet's Life* (1938), Masters was discovered to *Poetry* in August 1914 by Alice Corbin Henderson of the *Poetry* staff after reading his "Spoon River" poems in *Reedy's Mirror*—much to Monroe's chagrin that she should have been scooped in the discovery of a major Chicago poet by a St. Louis weekly, even though it was "our most progressive contemporary."³

But Harriet Monroe, already by this "miraculous" year the matriarch of Chicago's New Poetry Movement, gladly accepted Masters into her brood. In fact she claimed for her magazine and for Sandburg a greater debt from Masters than Masters himself ever admitted. She reminisces in *A Poet's Life* about some "personal confessions" in February 1915 among the *Poetry* group, of which Masters had become an enthusiastic member. "Edgar Lee Masters, for example, told how *The Spoon River Anthology* was conceived nearly a year ago, when his mind, already shaken out of certain literary prejudices by the reading in *Poetry* of much free verse, especially that of Carl Sandburg, was spurred to more active radicalism through a friendship with that iconoclastic champion of free speech, free form, free art—freedom of the soul."[4] She may have been right. We can almost feel Masters in *Across Spoon River* trying to put down accurately the friendship with Sandburg, all the while resenting him fiercely, for literary jealousies had long since estranged them.

But they were close friends throughout the composition of the "Spoon River" poems as they appeared in *Reedy's Mirror*. In November 1914 the *Mirror* printed Sandburg's poetic tribute to Masters, "To Webster Ford."[5] When Masters was ill early in 1915, Sandburg came to visit him one evening, but when told his friend was too ill for visitors he put himself to use helping Mrs. Masters do the dishes (*ASR*, 357). Later, though Masters says Sandburg's friendship had cooled by now, Sandburg and Harriet Monroe came to watch his prowess as a lawyer as he won a difficult court case; and immediately afterward, still in the summer of 1915, Masters, as he claims in *Across Spoon River*, took Sandburg's *Chicago Poems* with him to New York in a vain attempt to find them a publisher (*ASR*, 365–69).

Though Sandburg was ten years younger, Sandburg and Masters had both been ardent Populists at the beginning of their literary careers. Both had spent their early years in small Illinois towns— in fact, Sandburg's home town was Galesburg, where Masters had attended Knox College for a year. Probably most important for their relationship, both were writing poems in Chicago at a time when a confluence of people and events had made Chicago the new literary center of the country. They were participating in a dual literary and historical phenomenon which, in its local manifestation, came to be called the Chicago literary renaissance, and in its later and larger manifestation, the poetic renaissance of about 1912–20. Both Sand-

burg and Masters were writing out their Midwest experience: the
new Midwesterner Sandburg, the son of immigrants, and the old
Midwesterner Masters, grandson of pioneers. Both became famous,
and in their collective wake left a renewal of American poetry.

William Marion Reedy

Among Masters's acquaintances Dreiser—and to a degree Sandburg from about April 1914 to April 1915—replaced Ernest
McGaffey as a literary friend and stimulus, someone who had already
arrived and could offer both help in finding publishers and the
encouragement of one writer to another. But Reedy replaced Masters's boyhood "chum" Mitch Miller as bosom friend and confidant.
Their friendship was "the outstanding friendship of my life, as it
was of his," Masters wrote in one of his articles on Reedy after his
friend's death in 1920.[6]

Besides calling the attention of Masters to the *Greek Anthology,*
and perhaps giving it to him, Reedy evidently continued to remind
Masters of its excellence. Masters wrote in reference to the *Greek
Anthology* that he remembered "distinctly" Reedy's allusions to it
in the *Mirror.*[7] It is difficult to overstress the importance of this
book as a source of *Spoon River Anthology.* Willis Barnstone, in his
introduction to the 1968 edition of Masters's *Across Spoon River,* has
pointed out that the *Greek Anthology* provided not only the title
substantive "Anthology." It provided also the concept of a book of
epitaphs as well as the mood and form Masters's book was to take,
including gnomic epitaphs spoken from the grave in the first-person
singular, the use of interrelated voices in a series of plots, his emphasis on "sun and darkness—and more darkness than sun"—and
even his frankness "about every kind of sexual activity."[8]

Yet the real service of Reedy to Masters was professional and
editorial. Reedy had printed a few of Masters's early poems, probably
in the way of encouragement, as was his custom with writers he
thought might have promise. But in the early spring of 1914 he
returned a sheaf of poems to Masters unpublished, with editorial
advice. The *Mirror* was at this time Masters's only literary outlet,
since the musical weekly which had given him favorable attention
in Chicago had been closed to him late in 1911 under pressures
resulting from the Tennessee Mitchell affair (*ASR,* 314–15). So
Masters valued highly the availability of the *Mirror*'s columns, which
now seemed to be closing with the rejection of his verses.

There are several versions of the incident. In 1933, in "The Genesis of Spoon River," Masters wrote that he had been publishing in the *Mirror* rhymed poems in conventional meters. But Reedy's criticisms continually stressed that Masters should write from his own "experience and background" and that he could produce "more distinctive" work (48). In fact, T. K. Hedrick, associate editor of the *Mirror* at this time, reports that Reedy told Masters, "For God's sake, lay off" the kind of thing he had been doing.[9] Masters's version of the "genesis" continues with the recollection that when Reedy received the first Spoon River epitaphs, "his extravagant praise seemed like irony" to the "astonished" Masters. Masters had entitled the group of poems sardonically, "Spoon River Anthology." When he discovered that Reedy "really liked the work," he tried to change the title to "Pleasant Plains Anthology"; but Reedy's vigorous dissent prevailed (48–49).

In *Across Spoon River* Masters makes no mention of Reedy's role, but tells a story of a visit by his mother about 20 May 1914 and long talks with her about Lewistown and Petersburg characters, with the psychological effect of inspiring him to write the first Spoon River poems immediately upon her departure, as the first in a series of related poems—the structure of the novel he had thought of in 1906, but expressed in verse (*ASR*, 338–39). He then comments, as in the "Genesis of Spoon River" article, on his use of the pseudonym, Webster Ford, and he adds that only his own family, his secretary, and Sandburg, and later the editors of *Poetry*, knew he was the author. He does not mention Tennessee Mitchell, who would have recognized the name as that of the author of *Songs and Sonnets* (1910) and *Songs and Sonnets, Second Series* (1912), two books which she doubtless owned and which should have been, but were not, dedicated to her. He also neglects to mention Dreiser, whom he was keeping apprised of his progress on the *Anthology*.

Although Masters scanted Reedy in *Across Spoon River*, two years later, in 1938, Macmillan (which had published *Spoon River* and the later books through *Selected Poems*, 1936) published the autobiographies of two close friends of Masters, the editors of *Poetry*, Harriet Monroe and Eunice Tietjens. Both give accounts of the Reedy editorial rejection. Monroe in *A Poet's Life* says that, "Because his friend Reedy had refused his classic tales in verse and begged him to get up to date in style and subject, he had begun *Spoon River* as a kind of challenge to the free-versifiers. . . . Intending perhaps a parody, he was soon caught up by his subject."[10] Tietjens in *The World at My Shoulder* writes:

> The way of his release was this. I give it here because he told it to me while it was still burning in him. He . . . kept trying to persuade Reedy to publish . . . his poems. But Reedy, a man of fine literary perceptions, would have none of them. And he rallied Masters.
>
> "Why," he asked him in substance, "do you keep on writing these foolish watery lyrics and these remote fulminations? You know life. . . . Why don't you write about life as you know it? . . . something with guts in it?"
>
> And something answered in Masters one day, some burst of creative energy engendered by rage. . . . "You want life?" he answered. "Very well, you shall have life, and by God you shall have it raw!"
>
> So he went home . . . and began *Spoon River,* not thinking of the sketches as poetry, thinking of them as a means of refuting Reedy. But this astute editor recognized them for what they were and published them at once.[11]

Just before her book appeared, Tietjens checked with Masters, sending him relevant excerpts and later a copy of her book.[12] He never offered any refutation of her account of Reedy's role.

Reedy's own version he printed in the *Mirror* for 20 August 1915. "First, half piqued at my rejection of his efforts in accepted verse forms, he hurled at me three of the poems"—actually there were seven in the first group that Reedy printed, and he had earlier printed five of the conventional ones—"with a satiric query that perhaps this was what I liked. I printed them. He was surprised, half suspecting I was guying him."[13]

The point here is that the poems were not premeditated, that Reedy bullied and then shocked Masters into a form and content he might not have discovered otherwise. Not that the form and content were uncongenial; the voice of those "foolish watery lyrics" and those "remote fulminations"—to repeat Eunice Teitjens's apt phraseology—was not his. It was, to use another perceptive phrase from Tietjens's book, "Shelley seven times removed."[14] Masters was not the first poet, nor the last, to discover a congenial form or content through imitation, even though the imitation might be pastiche, parody, or burlesque.

If Reedy found for Masters a voice and made him famous, Masters with the success of *Spoon River Anthology* enlarged Reedy's audience

and gave him wide renown as an editor and critic. Each was permanently grateful to the other. Masters showed his affection and
gratitude in articles on Reedy, the "Literary Boss of the Middle
West," as he titled one; in poems, two of which bear Reedy's name;
and in his introduction to *Toward the Gulf,* a fond and grateful
appreciation of the editor who "inspired and instructed" him and
who assisted in "sculpturing the clay" taken from "the soil" of their
common midwestern origin (xii).

Reedy's appreciation for Masters, like Masters's for Reedy, was
for the man himself. Although the success of *Spoon River Anthology*
redounded to Reedy's increased prestige as well as to his financial
well-being, his greatest satisfaction came from the fact that he had
discovered in the Midwest, and in part made, a major literary figure.
Thereafter, Masters became in his relations to Reedy a sort of Galatea. Reedy, the critical artist, so admired what he had wrought—
Masters and *Spoon River Anthology*—that he became their defender
and their apologist. In part this role was forced on him by the
critical storm that the poems provoked when he published them in
the *Mirror.* Nevertheless, his biographer Max Putzel believes that
he made for Masters a unique exception in his normally judicious
critical procedures.

The Greek myth does not inform us how the perfection of Galatea,
the woman brought to life by the gods from the statue carved by
the sculptor Pygmalion, affected the artist's later career and work;
but the story indicates that he became, probably, a better human
being, if less an artist. After *Spoon River* Reedy published nearly
everything Masters sent him—according to Putzel, "far too
much. . . . Reedy in fact abdicated his critical function."[15] Putzel
is no doubt correct in saying that their friendship, after 1914, was
damaging to the creative potential of both men. As long as Reedy
defended him and published his work, Masters felt that he was
approved by the man he considered the only real critic of the time,
and so had no need to worry about such peccadillos as prolixity,
archaic diction, preaching to his audience, or the niceties of poetic
technique. Yet two important facts remained: *Spoon River Anthology*
would never have existed without Reedy; and the two men discovered a profound and lasting friendship. These are achievements
which might mark any individual life as a success.

After Reedy's death in 1920 Masters was desolate. He went west
to St. Louis for the funeral, then stopped in Petersburg, less than

a hundred miles distant, to see Mrs. Miller, the eighty-five-year-old mother of his boyhood "chum" Mitch, whom Reedy had for a time replaced. Masters had just finished writing *Mitch Miller,* of which he said, "No book that I have written is closer to my heart."[16]

Reedy was to Masters more than mentor and friend. He was a brother (as only his lost brother Alex might have been), almost a god. In "William Marion Reedy" in *Songs and Satires* he wrote that Reedy seemed to him like "a lighthouse" which sends forth a beam of light which makes the speaker believe "it's God." In "The Death of William Marion Reedy" from *The Open Sea,* he wrote of their "mystic brotherhood" and addressed his departed friend as "my brother."

Chapter Five
Spoon River Anthology

Weaving the Garlands: Organic Structure

An anthology, as anyone with a desk dictionary knows, is a collection of epigrams, as in the Greek *anthology*, meaning flower gathering, from *anthos* or flower, plus *logio* or collecting, from the Greek *legein*, to gather, to say: as in *logos* or speech, word. Masters could not have chosen an apter term for the title of his *Spoon River* poems; and of course he did not have to search his dictionary to find it, since Reedy had presented it to him (at least the term, if not the Greek collection of epigrams). As a reader of Greek, who had become fascinated with the language in his year at Knox College and had read Homer annually ever since, he was fully aware of the meanings of the term.

And therefore he was fully cognizant of what constitutes an epigram—according to Webster "a short poem dealing concisely, pointedly, and often satirically with a single thought or event and often ending with an ingenious turn of thought." The definition is surprisingly close to the definitions and prescriptions for "poetry" promulgated at about this time by Ezra Pound and the imagists in Harriet Monroe's *Poetry*. In fact many readers of Masters's early Spoon River "anthologies," as he often called them, recognized the affinity and described them as "imagistic."

The first set of verses, published by Reedy on 29 May 1914, included the *Spoon River* poems "Hod Putt," "Ollie McGee," "The Unknown," "Cassius [Hueffer]," "Serepta the Scold" (later "Serepta Mason"), "Amanda [Barker]," and "Chase Henry," together with the introductory poem "The Hill." In addition to being epigrammatic, all are epitaphs, another Greek term, defined as "a brief statement commemorating or epitomizing a deceased person or something past."

These definitions and etymological notes are reminders of the implications, for Masters, of the form and conventions he was working within. These first seven epitaphs are short, averaging ten lines apiece. Each one tersely summarizes the life of the person named in the title. Each is spoken in the first person by the voice of the deceased. Each concludes with a kind of ironic commentary on, or a moral drawn from, the life of the speaker. There is a certain variation in the person or persons addressed, usually the living villagers of Spoon River.

For instance, Hod Putt, seeing others grow rich by illegal or immoral means, decided to ease his poverty by robbing a stranger and accidentally killed him in the process. Addressing no one in particular, he summarizes by understatement and ironic comparison: he and the banker "sleep peacefully" in adjacent graves. Ollie McGee, who feels that her husband's secret cruelty destroyed her, tells Spoon River, addressed as "you," that she is avenged since her husband's memory of her is now destroying him. Cassius, who has ironically been given Caesar's epitaph (from Shakespeare's play), speaks of the villagers impersonally as "they," complaining of the folly of epitaph carvers. Serepta addresses the villagers scornfully as "Ye living," who fail to perceive beauty and the controlling influences on human life. Amanda reveals to the passing "Traveler" that though the villagers believe her husband loved her, actually he killed her out of hate. The town drunkard, Chase Henry, gloats to the "pious souls" of the village that he has equal honor in death with the most prudent who lie beside him. The anonymous voice in "The Unknown" from an unmarked grave confesses to the hopeful his youthful brutality in wounding and caging a hawk; wounded and caged himself by life, he searches Hades to offer friendship to the soul of the bird. This poem adopts outright the Greek conceptions of soul and the afterlife.

These seven epitaphs set the pattern for all that were to follow, 212 in all in the first edition, not counting the fine introductory poem "The Hill" and the trivial blank-verse "Spooniad" at the end. Masters eventually added thirty-one new epitaphs for the "definitive" second edition, plus a rambling, superfluous epilogue in dramatic form which mingles mythological voices from various cultures (such as God, the Sun, Beelzebub, Yogarindra).

Reedy published the "anthologies" as they emerged from Masters's hand, typically jotted down between court sessions in the spring and fall of 1914, or composed at leisure at the rented summer place at Spring Lake, Michigan. For the most part, though the slips of paper from which they were typed by Jacob Prassel, Masters's secretary, were thrown away, we can guess from Masters's accounts of their composition and from his habitual practice that they were hastily written and sent off and published unrevised. Perhaps Jake Prassel or Reedy corrected the more obvious misspellings and typographical errors of the sort that litter Masters's correspondence and even some of his published works. A few that remain in later editions of *Spoon River* are the name "Dr. Siegrfied Iseman" in one of the thirty-one added poems; the solecism "bursted" in the poem "Gustav Richter," which is not otherwise dialectal; the misuse of the word "namesake" in "Percy Bysshe Shelley"; the inconsistent and misleading capitalization of "my Father" and "my Mother" in the poems "Cooney Potter" and "Nellie Clark" but not, for instance, in "Le Roy Goldman"; the placing out of order, in the alphabetized table of contents, of the added poems "Kinsey Keene" and "Sexsmith the Dentist." These are at worst venial sins of writing or proofreading; they do little damage to the poems. But they do reveal haste in composition and a greater concern with the idea of the character to be expressed than with the specific language in which it is conveyed.

When Reedy published the second group of poems on 19 June 1914, three weeks after the first group, he labeled them "A Second Garland," thus emphasizing the anthology motif as a gathering of flowers for the graves of the dead. He continued this usage through the later installments of the *Anthology*, comprising a total of twenty-six garlands, averaging eight or nine poems each and published over a period of thirty-two weeks, concluding with the single epitaph of the pseudonymous author "Webster Ford" on 15 January 1915. The second garland contained ten poems, averaging fourteen lines in length (compared to ten lines in the first garland). The third contained eleven poems averaging sixteen lines. The length of the poems did not increase drastically, however, as "Webster Ford" contains only thirty-one lines, and the longest epitaph, "Caroline Branson," has forty-five. Masters's apparent preference for the somewhat longer poem with greater room for descriptive detail and philosophic statement is exhibited in the work he published both before *Spoon River* and after, with the exception of *The New Spoon River* (1924) and *Lichee Nuts* (1930). Here, however, the epigrammatic and epitaphic forms constrained him to a very effective concision of statement and often ironic understatement.

As the poems appeared they developed into a gallery of individual portraits. All but six were titled with an individual name, and these six also presented particular persons: "The Unknown," "The Village Atheist," "The Town Marshall," "The Circuit Judge," "Many Soldiers," and "William and Emily." Sometimes other names would appear in a poem, or references to other persons. For instance Ollie McGee mentions her husband; Amanda Barker mentions her husband Henry; and Chase Henry mentions "the banker Nicholas" and "his wife Priscilla." But these other characters are left undeveloped. However, in the twenty-first anthology, "Judge Somers," published a month after the first garland, occurs the familiar name Chase Henry and the reminder that he was "the town drunkard." Thus the eminent judge joins the drunkard and the banker and his wife in ironic juxtaposition on the Hill. In the twenty-fourth anthology, "Nicholas the Banker"—or his ghost—appears in person ("Nicholas Bindle" in the book form of *Spoon River*) to mention his nemesis, the rival banker Deacon Rhodes.

In the fifth garland, published two months after the first, is the epitaph of A. D. Blood, including among other names the familiar one, from the first garland, of Benjamin Pantier. Here also is "Blind Jack" containing the names "Butch" Weldy, the rapist in "Minerva [Jones]" from the second garland, and Jack McGuire who had killed the murderous marshal of "The Town Marshal" in the third garland. In the sixth garland (7 August) appear the adjacent portraits "Doctor Meyers" and "Mrs. Doctor Meyers" (later simply "Doc Meyers" and "Mrs. Meyers"). Both, even from the grave, avoid explicit mention of the event which destroyed their lives, Doc Meyers's attempted abortion of Minerva Jones's fetus conceived in the rape by "Butch" Weldy. Here, after nearly fifty previous epitaphs, Masters has discovered and established the basic plan of his *Anthology*: interrelated lives and events from the fictional village of Spoon River with adjacent portraits commenting ironically on one another.

When he rearranged the epitaphs for publication in book form, Masters left the first two, "Hod Putt" and "Ollie McGee," at the beginning, but then placed immediately after "Ollie" the epitaph of Fletcher McGee, her husband, from the fifteenth garland, giving his side of the story, like hers truthful yet unregenerately hating. And Thomas Rhodes, the banker and arch villain of the book,

Masters mentioned in eight earlier epitaphs before allowing him to speak his own—smug, self-righteous, confident even in death—and finally included him in a total of twenty epitaphs. No other character is mentioned in more than five or six epitaphs, though about a dozen appear that frequently; this makes the banker Rhodes (probably named after the British financier Cecil Rhodes) the central cohesive force of the *Anthology* as he was of the village Spoon River. In the macrocosm he represents mammon worship.

Spoon River as portrayed in these epitaphs is no bucolic haven of peace and love. There are fond portraits of Masters's grandparents and their farm in the epitaphs of Davis and Lucinda Matlock and of the old pioneers, Masters's great-great-grandparents John and Rebecca Wasson. And there are frequent echoes of Masters's early years in Petersburg: for instance "little Paul," who was his beautiful little brother Alex, from the epitaph "Hamlet Micure," which is a pseudonym of Masters himself. Other instances are "Emily Sparks," modeled on an early teacher (with perhaps something added from the life of Mary Fisher, his teacher in the Lewistown high school); "Johnnie Sayre," who is Mitch Miller, killed while "flipping" a train and having his leg severed (he even has for the inscription on his stone the theme of Mitch's funeral sermon in the later novel, to the effect that his death saved him from "the evil" of an adult life). But most of the epitaphs come from Masters's Lewistown memories.

Thomas Rhodes from almost the center of the book (his is epitaph number 103 of 243) presents the division of the town into two groups, liberals and conservatives. Himself a proud conservative, banker, industrialist, churchgoer, and prohibitionist, Rhodes gibes at the liberals, poets, and intellectuals who he assumes have divided souls. Three epitaphs later, Jim Brown the stableboy, at the other end of the social ladder, discovers the same division—between those who prefer a good fiddle tune and those who intone hymns, those who are "for the people" and those who are "for money." He also discovers that the secret of the difference is in the people's attitudes toward sex—when the Reverend Peet and "the Social Purity Club" try to make him take the stallion Dom Pedro outside of town because it corrupts "public morals."

If there are more prohibitionist ministers like Abner Peet than doctors such as Doc Meyers and Doc Hill ministering to the suffering souls in Spoon River, if there are more vindictive judges and prosecutors than intercessors, if the liberals are usually frustrated, still they have the last word. At the exact center of the book, with 121 epitaphs preceding and following his, stands "Jonathan Swift Somers," for whom "The evil of the world [was] lighted up and made clear." Himself an intellectual, one of several who speak in the voice of Edgar Lee Masters, he is author of the concluding mock-heroic "Spooniad." Immediately preceding "The Spooniad" is the epitaph of Webster Ford, the author of *Spoon River Anthology*. He recalls an incident from his youth in the mystical "Sunset hour by the river" when he perceived the god Apollo, and his friend Mickey (Mitch, again) thought it a ghost, and the banker's son, Ralph Rhodes, made fun of them. He loses the vision but gains it again with a crown of laurel which he offers to the followers of the Apollonian way, those of heroic heart, "fearless singers and livers." Despite an unfortunate apparent reference to the internal organs, heroic hearts and "fearless livers" are a synecdoche, common in Masters, for the free and hearty people of Virginia as opposed to New England Calvinists.

As a whole the *Anthology* is an extraordinary gallery of saints and rogues, predominantly the latter. As a realistic novel, Masters's projected "only book" that he says he mentioned to his father in 1906, it is a convincing portrait of the small Midwestern town with its central square, its numerous churches, its proud opera house, its drug store and general store, its wagon works and canning factory or other new industry. Its interpreters, now dead, were its ordinary citizens, occupying the various trades and professions of the village, or farming on its outskirts. Since they have died, few are young, though many, like Webster Ford, speak to the youth of Spoon River.

The village is small enough that most of the townsfolk know one another. In fact they know a considerable amount about each other's lives, sometimes too much. And much of what they know, or think they know, turns out to be false, often rumor disseminated by the venal Editor Whedon of the *Spoon River Argus* or other scandal mongers looking for any sort of tawdry glitter to enliven their commonplace lives. At times this little knowledge proves disastrous, as to Doctor Meyers, indicted and disgraced for trying to help Minerva Jones, the village poetess. More frequently it causes a total misevaluation of a life, often symbolized by a hypocritical epitaph carved on a gravestone. And so the villagers speak in an effort to clarify their stories.

Sometimes their words are confessions, like that of Deacon Taylor, pillar of the church and supporter of prohibition, who died from thirty years of secret tippling. Sometimes they are self-justifications like that of Serepta Mason, who had shown only her stunted side to the village, or of "Indignation" Jones, father of Minerva, "Mired in a bog of life" by circumstance, and whose epitaph, incidentally, has one of the most convincing conclusions in the *Anthology*, as he reminds his readers in understatement that they knew him only by his footsteps as he went out to purchase his meagre "nickel's worth of bacon." Some of the epitaphs are simply explanations of a life, some offer a discovered truth to the living villagers, some inquire about persons or events of interest to them before they died. Charlie French wonders which of his playmates snapped the toy pistol against his hand so that he died of lockjaw; his epitaph has one of the least effective endings in the *Anthology*, as he sobs in self-pity, wondering at the perpetrator.

Besides the dramatic and dialectical relationships among the characters, there is a continuously expanding and contracting time line. Many of the characters might have died yesterday in a contemporary Midwestern village named Spoon River. Some, like John Wasson, lived at the time of the Revolution. And they speak at different times—usually to the living citizens of Spoon River, sometimes to one another, or to a loved one left behind. A. D. Blood, for example, complains that the milliner's daughter Dora Williams and Reuben Pantier at night use his grave as "their unholy pillow." Many years later Reuben having lived and died remembers only how the same Dora Williams "made me trouble"; and Dora remembers Reuben only as the first of many lovers. Similarly Ollie McGee knows that Fletcher McGee's memory of her is killing him; when he has died he confesses, in an oddly inappropriate and jingly regular rhythm, that she indeed haunted him to death. Although fairly convincing as dramatic situation, "Fletcher McGee" is one of the least convincing epitaphs, as a poem, and the most regular metrically. Masters knew and did much better; "Petit, the Poet" convincingly mocks such "faint iambics."

Pessimism and Affirmation: The Curse and Glory of Sex

In addition to being in some respects a realistic novel of Midwestern village life, *Spoon River* can be read as a naturalistic novel

of the forces—biological, social, economic, political, and others—
that control human life and limit human freedom and the efficacy
of the will. Of all the controlling forces the sex-drive seems dominant
in these stories. Margaret Fuller Slack, named after the famous
nineteenth-century American feminist and intellectual, concludes,
after a life exhausted in childbearing, that the sexual urge "is the
curse of life!" Professor Newcomer, who was actually Masters's mentor at Knox College, sees as a cosmic joke nature's giving to man
a brain and the potential for a spiritual life and then allowing him
no outlet for his creative talents but survival and sex.

Indeed, much of the early fame of *Spoon River* derived from its
sexual frankness. For many readers it provided merely titillation.
To others it was tasteless and shocking, though today its revelations
seem tame enough. To still other readers it was a welcome breath
of fresh air let into the stultifying oppressiveness of late Victorian
Comstockery. And probably for thousands the light shed in these
poems on sexual urges, practices, and repressions was truly a revelation through which they could find company in their misery and
relief from their sense of guilt. It is impossible to read the epitaph
of Nellie Clark, seduced by an older boy when she was only eight
and then whispered about and scorned because she was not a virgin
when she married, without condemning the narrow village morality
and hypocrisy. It is impossible to read very far in *Spoon River* without
discovering sex and its repression dominating a majority of lives.
In the epigraph poem "The Hill," the unknown speaker asks from
the grave, where now are five young girls of the town? He is answered
by the voice of omniscience, that three at least have died of "childbirth," of "thwarted love," or "in a brothel." Among the first
twenty-three epitaphs thirteen emphasize misdirected or frustrated
sexual energies.

Of course sexual and social repression are not the only limitations
that denied these speakers personal fulfillment while they lived.
There is much mention of Fate, or a personified "Life" that rules
their lives. Many speakers ascribe their failures to having been caught
in some sort of metaphoric trap. Robert Fulton Tanner—named
ironically for the inventor of the steamboat, which molded the
character of the whole Mississippi Valley—is caught metaphorically
in his own patent rat trap when he is bitten by a rat while dem-
onstrating the trap. So he likens himself to the rat, caught by "the
monstrous ogre Life." Cassius Hueffer rewrites his own epitaph,

saying that he found that "Life" was "not gentle." The outspoken, freethinking Wendell Bloyd speaks parenthetically of an envious, petty God, saying he believes God allowed His Son to be crucified, "because it sounds just like Him." Godwin James, who followed Christianity, still does not know whose face smiles at him hidden by a "demoniac mask." Sometimes the sins of the father are visited upon the child, as Lois Fluke Spears was born blind after her father Willard Fluke contracted venereal disease when he broke his marriage vows with the woman called Cleopatra. And we are back again with the controlling power of sex. Lois Spears, ironically, is one of the few to live a fulfilled life—for which she gratefully praises God.

Thus the general deterministic framework of Masters's naturalism is not wholly pessimistic. People are moved by forces which they can neither control nor understand. Calvin Campbell, named after the great exponent of theological determinism John Calvin, admonishes those "who are kicking against Fate" that it is their own will that makes of them weeds instead of flowers; and Louise Smith warns in another garden metaphor that one's will should not be allowed to "play gardener" to one's soul. Men and women are too limited in knowledge and power to make their wills effective. So they must trust their souls.

Here, beneath all the realistically portrayed squalor and misery, weakness, ignorance, greed, and sin, and beyond the pessimistic naturalism, is the bedrock affirmation of the *Spoon River Anthology*. It is Masters's basic faith in the sovereignty and immortality of the soul. Among these 243 epitaphs are at least 125 direct references to "soul" or "spirit." The souls that speak do not often seem to have attained the Truth. But they speak their own truths in, for the most part, their own voices. If there is a single theme to the *Anthology*, it is the old American-Jeffersonian theme of liberty: a plea for each individual to be granted the freedom to work out his own destiny, his salvation or damnation, with a minimum of political and social restraint.

Thomas Rhodes, leader of the conservatives, feels he has found salvation, "self-contained, compact, harmonized"; and John Cabanis, leader of the liberals, having deserted "the party of law and order," has found his truth in the vision of ultimate "Freedom," to be achieved speck by speck through the efforts of all who have fought for her. In between the two leaders (who are separated by only fifteen epitaphs), the stableboy Jim Brown simply observes the difference between the groups and concludes that it is all in how they regard sex. Fortunately Brown and Masters do not elaborate on that idea, one of the book's few examples of effective understatement. But the reader of the *Anthology* carries the secret further: the difference lies in the relative willingness or unwillingness of the two groups to allow individuals to seek their own salvations by following their own human needs and desires. On the left Carl Hamblin, editor of the *Spoon River Clarion*, had his press wrecked and was tarred and feathered for publishing an allegorical protest against the hanging of the Haymarket anarchists in Chicago, picturing Justice with eyes bandaged only to hide the corruption under the bandage. On the right Jacob Godbey, opponent of saloons, points the town liberals to their "goddess, Liberty, . . . a strumpet," who sells out the town to the big-city saloon owners.

The poet and critic Amy Lowell, in her influential *Tendencies in Modern American Poetry* (1917), calls Masters "more preoccupied with sex than any other English or American author has ever been."[1] Many have called him sex-obsessed. Yet what he is truly emphasizing in *Spoon River Anthology* is, first, the importance of sex as a basic and powerful human drive that may, like other powerful natural forces, become personally and socially dangerous if repressed and confined. Second, he tries to make us see that as a basic human need, sex is a function of liberty; to repress sexual expression is to deny an essential freedom.

Freedom therefore is the central theme of *Spoon River Anthology*, and sex is its central metaphor. Two additional epitaphs which exhibit this metaphor are those of Daisy Fraser and Lucius Atherton, who serve as a sort of comic chorus. Daisy, the village prostitute, keeps her own integrity, frequently donating "ten dollars and costs" to the local school fund. Lucius, preferably pronounced "luscious," gallivants his way through *Spoon River* until he is only, as he sadly confesses, an unkempt, greyhaired, "discarded, rural Don Juan." At the end of his epitaph he mentions the poet Dante and recognizes that "the force" that elevated Dante was the same that drove poor Lucius "to the dregs of life." That force, clearly, is the sexual impulse. In its higher manifestation it is human love; in its highest, divine or spiritual love. It is democratically available to all. Each individual can make of it and of himself, within the limitations of fate and circumstance, whatever his genius—or the laws and mores of the people about him—allows.

In the village morality of Spoon River, few can achieve sexual, which is to say human, self-realization. The school teacher Emily Sparks, "the old maid, the virgin heart," attains a kind of spiritual love for her pupil Reuben Pantier, but at the expense of physical love and human companionship. Trainor the druggist, in the epitaph following Emily's, observing the chancey chemistry of marital relations, remains a bachelor but is killed by an explosion of chemicals confined in a test-tube. Daisy Fraser, in the next epitaph, is exploited and abused by the town; capable of love, she is permitted only sex.

Even free love seems not to be the answer, perhaps because it may only be practiced in the impersonal city, in Chicago, Paris, London, or because even in the city repressive mores restrict its development beyond mere sex. Georgine Sand Miner, modeled on Tennessee Mitchell, though named this time for an earlier feminist, George Sand, practiced free love. Like Tennessee (Deirdre in *Across Spoon River*), she is the mistress of a married man whom she adores, Daniel M'Cumber (one of Masters's many aliases in *Spoon River*); she begs him to flee with her to another city, and upon his stating his preference to go on as they are, she confesses to his wife and so ends the affair to her own sorrow, wishing that her lover "had . . . shot me dead!" It is of interest to note in passing that she twice mentions "My Lesbian friend." There is no necessary implication that she herself is lesbian; but this appears to be Masters's one reference to homosexuality in the *Anthology*, which was once notorious for dealing with every sort of sexual activity. Although Masters refers to the subject of lesbianism elsewhere, particularly in *The Fate of the Jury* (1929), he barely mentions male homosexuality, except in his critical study *Whitman* (1937).

Traditionalism in Method and Meaning

Far from being a sex-obsessed radical and iconoclast, Masters in *Spoon River* is a proponent of traditional Jeffersonian values, strictly heterosexual relationships, and Christian love, all based in a fundamental individualism which includes a belief in personal immortality and a salvation determined by one's conduct in this life.

The epitaphs of some of the few who do achieve fulfillment indicate this less obvious positive side to *Spoon River*. "William and Emily," a joint epitaph (like one other, "Many Soldiers"), speaks of the "unison between souls" ideally matched, like Squire Davis

Masters and Lucinda Masters, doubtless the prototypes of this epitaph. Lois Spears, born blind, lived "the happiest of women," offering neatness and hospitality to others. These are virtues which Masters always associated with his grandmother. Fiddler Jones, who speaks one of the finest epitaphs, lives for the day, bringing joy to others, and he is free of regrets. Francis Turner, whose story is partly that of Masters's adolescent love, Margaret George, and partly that of Masters himself (as he tells of their romance in the novel *Skeeters Kirby*), attains nirvana through his selfless passion for his girl "Mary." "Rebecca Wasson," the epitaph of Masters's great-great-grandmother, tells of a full life and reunion with her husband after death; and "Lucinda Matlock" and "Davis Matlock" relate the admirable lives of Masters's grandparents and their "sweet repose," secure in "immortal life." Tennessee Shope has found salvation in asserting "sovereignty" over her "own soul." William Jones, modeled on Dr. Strode, Masters's scientific friend from Bernadotte, near Lewistown, a "lover of Nature," has passed to "endless life." "The Village Atheist" admonishes the living that immortal life "is not a gift" but "an achievement."

Many of the later epitaphs emphasize the hunger for immortality and its possible attainment. Three in particular are worth noting here as all three speak for Masters himself. Alfred Moir rejoices at the chance that took him to the city where he "happened" to see the book in the window . . . luring" him to buy it. The book of course—unspecified in the poem—is the volume of Shelley's poems that Masters later wrote about in *Across Spoon River* (76–77) as a major discovery in his life. Alfred Moir confesses that it saved his soul. Le Roy Goldman, the revivalist, has learned that there is a surer way to heaven than the way he preached. It is to be blessed by having lost a parent or grandparent who "lived life strongly" and who can "speak for you" before God. Here is Masters's faith that his old grandmother—portrayed as the strong–living Lucinda Matlock—will lead him to heaven. The final epitaph, "Webster Ford," the pseudonym of the author, recounts, as we have seen, the speaker's mystical guidance through and beyond life by "Delphic Apollo." Masters's future at this point seemed secure.

Despite the realism, the naturalism, the pessimistic voices of the dead speaking bitterly or ironically or pathetically of their failed lives; despite the sordid pictures of sexual frustration and marital incompatibility, Masters's fundamental emphasis in *Spoon River* is affirmative. As Sarah Brown affirms in an early epitaph (the thirty-second), through physical love she attained spiritual love and discovered that though there are no marriages in heaven, "There is love." As Marie Bateson affirms in a late epitaph (the thirty-second from the end), the way to heaven is not to be found only through obeying the Commandments, for "freedom" is essential, and following one's own "vision." Love and freedom will find the way.

These are wholly acceptable propositions, especially if they shine out from the squalor and moral darkness of Spoon River Town like a light from under a bushel. But homilies seldom make good literature. Even readers who speak of the Bible as literature praise the dramatic, metaphorical, and lyric qualities found in the Book of Job and the Song of Songs, and not the homiletic. The most affirmative epitaphs of *Spoon River*, therefore, are likely to be the least convincing. Among the early ones are "Emily Sparks" the loving teacher and "Sara Brown" the blind but perfect homemaker. Among the later ones are many epitaphs which contain explicit philosophy or advice and which fail to develop any sense of the character of the speaker. These are likely to contain such words as "soul" or "Life," as "the Almighty hand of Life" in "Many Soldiers," or "deathless destiny" from "William H. Herndon." Other typical abstractions from the last fifty epitaphs are the following, all occurring in midline: "the Secret," "the Mystery," "Truth," "Fate," "quest," "vision," "the Shadow," "a Presence," "the antennae of Thought," "the Comforter," "Mystic moons," and "Infinite Truth." Somehow associated with these pretentious abstractions is an equally pretentious diction made up of neoclassical epithets and poetic clichés: "umbrageous Elm," "betimes" " 'mid stricken fields," "hasting with swift feet," "lambent laurel."

This is not to say that all the later poems are failures. The epitaphs "John Wasson," "Anne Rutledge," "Rebecca Wasson," "Rutherford McDowell," "Hannah Armstrong," and "Lucinda Matlock"—all, incidentally, portraying the pioneer stock—are strong poems conveying a sense of character. And perhaps the eighteenth-century language and homily, which creep into these poems too, is appropriate to these eighteenth-century pioneers who were brought up on, and lived by, the Bible.

Chapter Six

Spoon River Before and After: Sources and Criticism

The Critics Respond

The commentary on *Spoon River Anthology* already given suggests some of the problems which faced the critics at the outset in the fall of 1914 after Reedy had published ten or twelve garlands in the *Mirror*. Many of the poems showed obvious disrespect for the dead, others disrespect for the living. Much of the free verse, as well as the novelistic narrative and plot elements, seemed more like prose than poetry. The poetry was too new fangled, except where it was too old fashioned. Much of it flouted conventional moral and religious values, and much of it was too explicitly moral and philosophic.

The first reviews, in *Current Opinion* and Harriet Monroe's *Poetry*, were both favorable, though somewhat tentative. Monroe always regretted that *Poetry* had not been the first to discover and publish Masters, who was Chicago's greatest claim to literary fame. But she consoled herself with the assurance that *Poetry* through Sandburg and the imagists had inspired Masters, and that *Poetry* had published the first review of the poems. Actually, as Masters points out in *Across Spoon River* (346), the September 1914 review in Edward J. Wheeler's *Current Opinion* appeared the month before Alice Corbin Henderson's notice in *Poetry* in October.[1] In any event, the importance of the claim to priority to Monroe indicates the extraordinary caliber of Masters's stock in 1915 and after. It did not matter that *Poetry* had published Lindsay, Sandburg, and Pound before *Spoon River Anthology* appeared, and Frost, Eliot, Stevens, and Williams during the poetic renaissance. In 1915 Masters was the poet of the year, with the *Anthology* proclaimed by *Publisher's Weekly* the year's "outstanding book—not only the outstanding book of poetry";[2] and he was poet of the next year as well, winning the Helen Haire Levinson Prize from *Poetry*'s panel of judges. He was virtually the poet of the century, *Spoon River* being ranked fourth among "The Ten Best Books of the Present Century" as selected for the *Literary Digest* in 1923 by its panel of literary critics.[3]

The *Spoon River Anthology*, in fact, had received unusual attention before it was even printed as a book in May 1915. *Reedy's Mirror* was widely read in America and abroad by the literary cognoscenti. Before 20 November 1914, when Reedy finally prevailed upon Masters to allow him to reveal the identity of Webster Ford, Reedy and "Ford" were receiving a large correspondence praising and sometimes reviling *Spoon River*.

Very soon individual poems were being reprinted with comment by journals such as *Current Opinion* and *Poetry* that exchanged their issues with Reedy. The *Mirror* itself had printed about a dozen articles and letters on "Spoon River" by May 1915; *Current Opinion* had printed four, *Poetry* two, the *Chicago Evening Post* two. The *New York Times*, the *Chicago Tribune*, the *Boston Evening Transcript*, the *New Republic*, the *Nation*, in England the *Egoist*, and numerous others had all taken notice of the book soon to emerge.[4]

In the critical essay which accompanied his announcement of Masters's identity in November 1914, Reedy echoed Masters's democratic Populist sentiments and deplored with him the loss of the old values of individualism and integrity. Yet like Masters he remained sanguine about the future, not so much because he had Masters's underlying faith in the human soul as because a poet, Masters, had arisen to lead the way.[5] As soon as Masters's identity was known, letters and visitors came directly to him; among the latter were the British critic John Cowper Powys and emissaries from various periodicals seeking interviews.

Powys had first read *Spoon River* when Dreiser had lent him the proof sheets of the book, with Masters's permission, in March 1915. Powys immediately appointed himself Masters's unofficial press agent in a series of lectures and articles ballyhooing the *Spoon River Anthology* and its author. The first of these was a New York lecture reported in the *New York Times*: "Spoon River Poet Called Great: Famous English Critic Lifts Edgar Lee Masters from Chicago Obscurity to the High Peak of Parnassus." Unlike more conservative critics, Powys called Masters a "really great poet." Like Reedy and most approving reviewers, he compared Masters with Whitman.

Masters was "the natural child of Walt Whitman." He was "the only poet with the true Americanism in his bones"; in fact, he was "the aboriginal American poet."[6]

In the same article was a report of an interview with Masters by the *Times* Chicago correspondent, who found him "broad shouldered and of athletic build," as well as a "modest and unassuming man very much wrapped up in his home and family." Here for the first time occurs Masters's novel theory of the genesis of *Spoon River*. Asked what inspired the work, Masters replied, "Well, I always had it in mind to write a novel about a small community, including every interest and every piece of machinery you find in the big world or metropolis. . . . "

Dreiser, despite his fear that excessive praise would be harmful, contributed to the réclame about Masters's poetic prowess. So did others whose opinions still count in literary matters. Among them were Carl Sandburg, Vachel Lindsay, Hamlin Garland, Amy Lowell, H. L. Mencken, and Ezra Pound (the last two with reservations). Sandburg wrote a poetic "Tribute to Webster Ford" published in November 1914 by Reedy.[7] Vachel Lindsay praised him in a speech at the Poetry Society Dinner in New York early in 1916.[8] Hamlin Garland invited Masters to contribute a weekly column of prose portraits to *Collier's* (*ASR*, 363). Amy Lowell included him as one of six poets she celebrated in her book *Tendencies in Modern American Poetry*, though she included him in a chapter with Sandburg and omitted Lindsay altogether, both to Masters's annoyance, as recounted in Monroe's *A Poet's Life* (*ASR*, 402).

On Christmas Eve 1914 H. L. Mencken wrote to Masters expressing his interest in the *Anthology* and asking for a copy, as he had earlier asked Reedy to let him print original *Spoon River* epitaphs in the *Smart Set*.[9] Mencken in his *Prejudices: First Series* (1919) summarizes his opinion of Masters, "for a short season the undisputed Homer of the [new poetry] movement": "His undoubted merits in detail—his half wistful cynicism, his capacity for evoking simple emotions, his deft skill at . . . *vers libre* . . ."; and his "defects . . . in his later books"—"empty doggerel," unpoetical poetry, and "very bad tracts."[10]

Ezra Pound first commanded that Monroe "GET SOME OF WEBSTER FORD'S STUFF FOR 'POETRY!' "[11] He then published the *Egoist* article, "Webster Ford," in which he exclaimed "At last! At last America has discovered a poet," and he reprinted two of the best poems from

"Spoon River," "Doc Hill" and "The Hill."[12] Pound even tried, in his enthusiasm, to find merit in "Mr. Ford's 'Songs and [S]onnets, second series,' " but gave up with the remark, "but what is the use of discussing faults which a man has already discarded." About the time this short essay was published (January 1915), Pound was writing another, longer essay after having read more of the *Spoon River* poems as they appeared. This essay, which he sent directly to Masters in April 1915, was cautionary.

The cautionary portion of Pound's article, "Affirmations: Edgar Lee Masters," contained suggestions as to how to "make a book" of the poems: "a rather strenuous revision," and "a few months of meditation wherein to select from the rather too numerous poems." Pound was very aware of dangers: "If . . . he grows facetious, or lets down the tone, relaxes his seriousness, grows careless of rhythm, does not develop it, allows his method to become mere machinery, 'systematizes his production,' then one will have to register another disappointment."[13] Reedy printed the article six weeks later in the *Mirror*. But the *Spoon River Anthology* was already published. It had been in proof since January. Pound printed a few *Spoon River* epitaphs in his *Catholic Anthology* (1915), but it was apparent that his warnings had not been heeded in the *Spoon River* volume. When Masters's *The Great Valley* and *Songs and Satires* appeared the next year, Pound concluded that their author had "gone off into gas."[14]

Yet in 1915 the praise appeared nearly unanimous, for every negative appraisal seemed to call forth multiple defenses, sometimes a defense by the original doubter. W. S. Braithwaite, the conservative critic who thought *Spoon River* a "fascinating novel" in May 1915, was dubious about its poetic value. By January 1916 he had concluded that *Spoon River Anthology* "is the skillful welding together of the arts of the poet and the novelist . . . a unique as well as a great contribution to American literature."[15] Lawrence Gilman in an essay entitled "Moving Picture Poetry" praised the *Anthology* for its "rapidly shifting visualizations" and its events "exhibited from different dramatic angles" as on the screen, then closed with the animadversion, "But why drag in poetry?"[16]

Willard Huntington Wright, one of the *Anthology*'s most vehement detractors, insisted that, "As art, in the true sense, it is nonexistent." He discounted Masters as a poet in *Spoon River* because "His lines repudiate scansion, as he himself repudiates rhyme." The book lacked originality, since Edwin Arlington Robinson "did it better twenty years ago." Wright's strictures, in the January 1916 *Forum*, evoked a reply in an editorial in the *New York Sunday Times* for 2 January 1916, praising Masters's work as "Browningesque in its strength, originality, and satiric quality."[17]

Some of the most energetic debate appeared in the letters sections of various literary periodicals. In the *Dial* for March, April, May, and June 1916 a spirited interchange occurred between two literate gentlemen, Orvis Irwin and Roger Sherman Loomis, the former initiating aspersions on the *Anthology* and the latter offering prompt ripostes. In the letters column of *Reedy's Mirror*, Ezra Pound came to mingle with the hoi polloi in Masters's defense—or more accurately came to attack conservative critics—in 1915.[18]

For it was not only the near unanimity of critical opinion that affected Masters. It was equally the voice of the people, expressed in letters to editors and in sales figures of the *Mirror* and of editions of *Spoon River Anthology* that impressed him. Writing his autobiography in 1935, he said that what had enthralled him in Whitman, from his days with Margaret George in Lewistown, was Whitman's celebration of a future America with a new democratic art, in which Whitman would play the role of Hesiod and some poet still to come the role of Homer (*ASR*, 336). Clearly Masters aspired to be the American Homer. Whitman had failed to reach the people with his message of democratic truth. Masters in *Spoon River* began to reach them.

The Question of Sources

In light of the book's underlying philosophy and to the extent that Masters succeeded in reaching his proper audience (whether or not he originally aimed at it), the quibbles of the critics about the sources of *Spoon River* and whether it was truly poetry are irrelevant. Yet to Masters they were not irrelevant, and he took some pains to answer them. Both quibbles may be seen in the criticism of W. H. Wright, just cited: the lack of poetic quality and the indebtedness to E. A. Robinson. Wright's definition of poetry is relevant to Masters's response: "Here and there . . . an inversion, a thoughtful simile, . . . rhythm or assonance."

Nearly a year before Wright's 1916 *Forum* essay, Masters had taken up the subject with his usual industry and lawyer's passion for discoverable facts. The result of these researches was "What Is

Poetry?"[19] In his article Masters proposes that the principal criterion is not inversions or similes but invention.

Whether the *Anthology* answered the criterion of invention was a question not often asked, though other readers besides Wright noticed the book's similarities to the work of Robinson and the eighteenth-century English poet George Crabbe, usually with no imputation of plagiarism. Pound, for instance, indicating his disappointment with the too hasty publication of *Spoon River*, wrote in the *Little Review* for August 1916 that "What is good in it is good in common with things in the Greek Anthology, Villon and Crabbe."[20] The reference to Villon was to the fifteenth-century French poet François Villon and his forthright depiction of his own time, as well as his use of the *ubi-sunt* convention in his most famous line, "Où sont les neiges d'antan?"—"Where are the snows of yesteryear?" Masters echoes this convention in the first line of the *Anthology*, from "The Hill," "Where are Elmer, Herman, Bert, Tom and Charley . . . ?" and gives a more specific allusion in Petit the poet's reminder about "the snows . . . of yesterday."

At one of her salons, Masters says in his autobiography, Mrs. William Vaughn Moody, widow of the poet, commented on the similarity between *Spoon River* and the work of Edwin Arlington Robinson. Masters's explanation is that he had read E. C. Stedman's *American Anthology* (1900) carefully but could not remember encountering Robinson's name or any of his poems, though Mrs. Moody detected a resemblance to Crabbe in both Robinson and Masters (*ASR, 372*).

In "The Genesis of Spoon River" (43), Masters comments on these critical references to Crabbe, saying that when critics perceived a resemblance he bought Crabbe's poems to read "for the first time," as he had never opened "the old book" in the Masters home. Masters presents himself as an omnivorous reader all his life, especially of poetry, and he lists Crabbe's poems as one of only seven volumes in his home in Lewistown (considering "a few plays of Shakespeare" as a single volume). It seems scarcely credible that he should have missed Crabbe, except for an interesting aside inserted here. One of the volumes was an illustrated *Album of Authors* which he "read to tatters," studying the portraits of the authors and picking Shelley and Goethe "as the best of all." Shelley and Goethe became his lifelong favorites, the two authors, he says in "The Genesis of Spoon River" (42) and elsewhere, that most affected his life. He also tells here of his practice in the high school of inventing pretexts to use the school encyclopedia so that he could read in it the biographies of famous writers (43). Quite probably Crabbe was not represented in the *Album of Authors* and but sparsely if at all in the encyclopedia. It is quite possible, since Masters also refers to being inspired to read an author by the poet's portrait or his biography, that he was indeed never stimulated to open "the old book" in his home.

Certainly Robinson was not represented in any of the old books. But it seems unlikely that Masters would not have read an emerging poet of his own age. In *Across Spoon River* he constantly compares himself to other poets—Keats, Shelley, Wordsworth, Whitman—with respect to childhood homes, family support, poetic accomplishment at a given age (the comparison always stresses the peculiar obstacles in his own path).

In "The Genesis of Spoon River" Masters remarks tht he did not much care for Crabbe when he finally read him (43). In *Across Spoon River* he compares Robinson's poems unfavorably to William Vaughn Moody's (372). Furthermore, some fifty pages earlier, bemoaning his lack of support as a poet in Chicago, he writes that two early books, *Songs and Sonnets* (1910) and *Songs and Sonnets, Second Series* (1911) and Robinson's *The Town Down the River* (1910) were reviewed in the Boston newspapers "side by side" (315). Robinson's fourth book of poems *The Town Down the River* is inexplicably indexed in *Across Spoon River* as a work by Edgar Lee Masters. Certainly Masters must have taken some note of this New England competitor at least by 1910.

The point here is not that Masters borrowed from Robinson the concept of the town microcosm and the technique of brief acidulous portraiture. The point is that he should have been at such pains to deny it. He took later at least equal pains to deny the influence of Robert Browning, particularly that of Browning's *The Ring and the Book* upon Masters's *Domesday Book* (1920). Browning is not even included in the alphabetical index of *Across Spoon River*, although there are at least three separate references to his name (118, 369, 408), the second of these indexed under *"Ring and the Book."* An explanation is that Masters may have valued too highly invention as an artistic criterion, or that he misinterpreted it. Clearly he believed in genius, and at least after 1914 he believed in his own muse or "daemon" or "brother god" or "star," which might visit him with inspiration. Despite the great breadth of his reading and knowledge, he may not have realized how much the greatest artists borrow from their predecessors and steal from their contemporaries. He may well have doubted his own method, which was essentially pastiche.

Dreiser, in a letter to Mencken of 20 July 1914 commending the *Spoon River* poems to Mencken's attention, wrote, "When an American poet—a writer of short poems arises I instantly think of . . . Thomas Hardy's brooding volumes and A. E. Housman (*The Shropshire Lad*)."[21] Masters's use of the term "A Moulder," who casts humans in their respective molds in the epitaph "Ippolit Konovaloff," is strongly suggestive of Hardy's many personifications of fate. In the epitaph "'Benjamin Pantier'" he has the dead owner speak sentimentally of his faithful dog, though without the ironic undercutting of the sentimentality in Hardy's "Ah, Are You Digging on My Grave?" (in which the dog replies that it was merely burying a bone and had "quite forgot" its dead mistress). These two poems were written about the same time and probably neither directly influenced the other.

As indicated earlier, Housman's *A Shropshire Lad* (1896) is echoed in the rhythm and intent of the opening question of "Hare Drummer," which brings to mind Housman's "Is My Team Plowing?" The next poem, about "Conrad Siever" who moves with "the chemic change and circle" of the earth's rotation, echoes Housman's "The Night Is Freezing Fast," whose fortunate hero has "woven a winter robe" against the cold, "And wears the turning globe."

There are echoes as well of John Masefield's *The Everlasting Mercy* (1911), which is itself indebted to Housman. Masefield's poem was notorious at the time for its presentation of "low" characters in their colloquial diction. More specifically, Masefield's long narrative poem anticipates the narrative or novelistic quality of *Spoon River*, and the mock-epic flights of the "Spooniad" may have an antecedent in Masefield's antagonists who fight for the right to poach.

Twenty-five years after *Spoon River*, Masters provided an unconscious hint of one of his sources in the quasi-biography *Emerson* (1940), where he remarks, "One of my favourite poems is 'Hamatreya.' " He prints twenty of Emerson's poems in their entirety and quotes from others, but oddly not from "Hamatreya." Emerson's poem opens with a list of New England names in the *ubi-sunt* formula: "Bulkeley, Hunt, Willard, Hosmer, Meriam, Flint / . . . Where are these men? Asleep beneath their grounds." Master's "The

Hill" begins with a similar iteration of names in a six-stress line, and similarly answers the rhetorical question—they are all "sleeping on the hill."

Dreiser himself is apparent not only in the naturalism of *Spoon River* and the epitaph "Theodore the Poet," but in the resemblance of "Flossie Cabanis" to Dreiser's *Sister Carrie* and in the reference to Charles T. Yerkes in "Adam Weirauch." Similarly a memorable phrase from Whitman (perhaps via Willa Cather's *O Pioneers*, 1913) is inserted into the middle of "Aaron Hatfield," whose speaker apostrophizes "you, O pioneers." One is reminded even of Emily Dickinson, whom Masters says he greatly respected as early as 1914 (*ASR*, 242–43). Her possible influence is felt in the gnomic quality of the epitaphs, the preoccupation with death, the frequent garden imagery, and even the name Emily occurring in two titles, "Emily Sparks" and "William and Emily."

The conclusion of "Anthony Findlay," with its opposition of the "wise" and "Strong" to the "weak" and "dull" and with its galloping anapests, has the tone and rhythm of Kipling. Thomas Gray's famous elegy written in a quite different country churchyard is strongly evoked by the lines in "Jonathan Houghton" about the tinkle of a distant cowbell and the "plowman on Shipley's Hill." Browning is everywhere suggested in the dramatic monologues of many epitaphs, with their truncated blank verse (unrhymed iambic tetrameter), often revealing ironically more of a speaker's less desirable traits than he means to tell. Two Browningesque unpremeditated murders are told in "Barry Holden" and "Searcy Foote." The name Browning appears in the penultimate poem of the *Anthology*, the mystical-philosophical "Elijah Browning."

In "Mrs. Williams" the lilting amphibrachs of W. S. Gilbert's operetta *Pinafore* (in which Masters saw his parents perform in Lewistown, with his mother in the role of Buttercup [*ASR*, 36]) are cleverly mimicked. The poem includes verbatim a line from "Little Buttercup," "Tŏ sét ŏff | swĕet fácĕs," which makes the allusion clear.

Tennyson's "Tears, Idle Tears" is specifically referred to in the *Spoon River* poem "Hamlet Micure," and Tennyson himself, as "Alfred." In the later volume, *The New Spoon River* (1924), a phrase from Tennyson's "The Eagle" appears without quotation marks in "Albert Thurston"—"who clasps the crags in lonely heights." Shelley also is specifically referred to in the *Anthology*. His name is first used in the epitaph title, "Percy Bysshe Shelley," whose story and monument are those of an actual boy, William Cullen Bryant, named for the American poet. Shelley occurs again, as a guardian spirit, in the mystical conclusion to the longest epitaph of the *Anthology*, "Caroline Branson," whose speaker implores "Shelley" to save her. He occurs as well in the poem "Gustav Richter," and in "Alfred Moir," already alluded to as the account of Masters's purchase of Shelley's poems as a young man.

Of course all writers, especially poets, write with some consciousness of a tradition, some knowledge of other writers whom they admire or have learned from. Consciously or unconsciously they imitate, borrow, plagiarize. But not all have been blessed with as retentive a memory as Masters's. Tietjens, who knew him and other famous writers over many years, wrote in *The World at My Shoulder*, "His conversation had—and still has—the greatest range of any I know." (Many of his admirers, Monroe, Sandburg, Powys, stress the wonder of his conversation.) "He had read everything, history, literature, law, science, and remembered it all."[22] So that if an idea, a character, an event occurred to him, it was likely to be in a formulation or phrasing he had heard or read.

Not being a notable phrasemaker himself, he quite naturally used the best phrasings available to him—as he used the best ideas, the best philosophies. All this is quite within the tradition of American eclecticism. The speaker in "Priam Finish," one of Masters's alter egos in *The New Spoon River*, and like Masters a seeker and a believer in human brotherhood, complains that the Old Testament is no better than it is, with its repetitions of conventional wisdom; and he asks, "How . . . then" should he be censured for his own use of pastiche—quotations, selection, reorganization? He might have added that the selection and reorganization are invention.

Chapter Seven
Other Directions in Poetry
Memories into Verse

On 15 January 1915, Edgar Lee Masters published his own epitaph as "Webster Ford" in *Reedy's Mirror*. *Spoon River* was finished: a few days later Masters was desperately ill with pneumonia.

With the help of a devoted nurse, Bertha Baum (Jane in *Across Spoon River*), and his own latent resiliency, his ever-renewed will to live, Masters recovered in a few months from his pneumonia. But he never recovered from the success of *Spoon River Anthology*. And he never fully understood it. While the praises and approbation of the book were still building, Masters was objecting to his friends that he could do better, nay had done better, in a direction quite different from *Spoon River*.

Almost immediately the publishers were clamoring for another book, though Macmillan's agent Edward Marsh warned Masters that the critics would be after him to prevent his repeating the literary coup of *Spoon River* (*ASR*, 366). Masters soon obliged with *Songs and Satires* (1916) and *The Great Valley* (1916). At the time, he was writing additional *Spoon River* poems and the epilogue for the definitive edition (1916). His close friend Eunice Tietjens remembers: "He would always in those days pull out a few more *Spoon River* sketches from his pocket and read them to us. And he used to look at me with a puzzled expression showing through his very justifiable pride, and ask: 'But why are these so much better than my other things? What makes people praise these and pay no attention to the others?' I tried to explain, but even then I could see it was no use. He could not understand."[1]

Harriet Monroe, writing her memoirs at the same time as Tietjens, had similar recollections: "He was the worst self-critic I have ever known." Tietjens wrote: "He has been blest with little or no literary judgment." Monroe: "After the success of *Spoon River* . . .

[when] he came to our office to show me the proofs of a proposed second book, I was aghast at discovering that he proposed to open it with the Launcelot and Elaine narrative of his ineffectual earlier period. My protest was emphatic. I can still see the puzzled look on his face." This second book for Macmillan, *Songs and Satires,* indeed took a quite different direction from *Spoon River*—the direction of "his ineffectual earlier period." Half its poems he had published before 1912. Heeding Harriet Monroe's pleas, Masters opened the book with the poem "Silence," first published by *Poetry,* and often anthologized. "But even so," she noted, *"Songs and Satires,* like many another second book made up largely from storage after a success, was a disappointment to critics and public, a fact which the author deeply resented and his friends deplored."[2]

Even "Silence," a Whitmanesque poem of seventy lines, sounds more like one of Sandburg's better poems than like the best of *Spoon River*. And it ends somewhat sententiously with "the silence" of those who have died and the lesson that it "shall be interpreted" to us as we "approach" our own deaths. In "The Vision," as early as page eighteen of *Songs and Satires,* we have a stream flowing "amidst our well beloved vale," and we are off not only in a different direction but in a different century of the past. If we persevere, we come near the end to the Launcelot narrative, written in imitation of medieval diction, with which Masters proposed to introduce his book. The knight visits the dead queen, kisses "the ceréd cloth," observing in "his woe" the perfection of her features, for "her nose was clear as snow." We forbear further comment.

The critics' disappointment is no surprise, though Masters's deep resentment is. As a man of his time, Masters evidently agreed with the critics who disliked *Spoon River* that poetry should generally adhere to a regular metric, such as the blank verse and ballad stanza of the two poems mentioned just above; that rhyme is desirable; that the diction should be "poetic," including frequent inversions. Masters's surprise at Reedy's acceptance of his first epitaphs and his perplexity at the critics' preference for his *Spoon River* poems was quite genuine. To him the *Anthology* really was in a direction quite other than what he considered his natural bent as a poet.

Nevertheless, with its publication he had crossed Spoon River, as imposing a stream figuratively as Caesar's Rubicon. He could not turn back. He was right in assuming that his gaining a reputation as a poet would ruin his legal practice. After *Spoon River* he had one large case; that was all, though he maintained a law office in the Loop in Chicago until 1920. The success of *Spoon River* committed him to a role as poet. He now turned his prodigious energy to filling the role and to finding the other direction in which his true talents lay. In the succeeding quarter century he published twenty volumes of poetry, seven novels, seven biographies (if we include studies of Whitman and Emerson, in which he allows his subjects to speak largely for themselves), and wrote at least twelve plays (two of them performed at colleges), and two historical studies. All of them were competent and none was much more than that.

Masters himself, he says in "The Genesis of Spoon River" (55), a comment reiterated in his son's "Biographical Sketchbook,"[3] preferred *Domesday Book* and its sequel *The Fate of the Jury* to his famous *Anthology*. The novel *Mitch Miller* was the book closest to his heart. *Lincoln, the Man* (1931) attained a certain notoriety. His biography of his friend, Vachel Lindsay, is still respected for its sincerity and honest portraiture; *The New World* (1937), which he called "The New Atlantis" before publication, was to be his masterpiece, the fruition of his lifelong goal "to epicize America."

Meanwhile a variety of currents were swirling about him, affecting his drift. World War I had begun in the summer of 1914, as the first *Spoon River* epitaphs were appearing in the *Mirror*. Masters, his secretary Jacob Prassel, Dreiser, and Mencken were all pro-German; but the United States was drifting toward support of Great Britain and the declaration of war on Germany in 1917. In the summer of 1915 Dreiser had prevailed upon Masters to visit New York, where he was lionized and celebrated as he never was in Chicago. He was growing dissatisfied with Chicago and contemplating moving to New York.

Part of his unrest was his growing dissatisfaction with his home life. No doubt in the background was Masters's more or less continuous philandering, of which he speaks frankly and with some relish in his autobiography and in his correspondence. There also was his first wife's natural objection to her loss of authority in her own home to Masters's attractive nurse Bertha Baum during his long illness in 1915 (the nurse slept in the room with her patient and excluded Mrs. Masters and visitors). Masters's inability to comprehend the doubts of others toward himself or his work is indicated in his final comment in *Across Spoon River* on the matter of his nurse. He is still, he protests, at a loss to understand his wife's dislike of

Bertha, for she had no cause at all for jealousy (*ASR, 359*). In the summer of 1917 Masters finally walked out on his wife and children.

On the literary scene, Robert Frost's *North of Boston* had appeared in 1914 while the *Anthology* was running in the *Mirror.* So had Vachel Lindsay's *The Congo* and Amy Lowell's *Sword Blades and Poppy Seeds.* Sinclair Lewis published *Our Mr. Wrenn,* his second novel; but not until he followed Masters's lead in *Main Street* (1920), his seventh novel, did he attain real success. In 1915 Sherwood Anderson read *Spoon River* and set to work on *Winesburg, Ohio* (1919); and Anthony Comstock, at the height of his power as self-appointed guardian of the public morals, died—probably not as a direct result of reading the "sex-obsessed" *Spoon River Anthology.* In 1916 came Robinson's *The Man Against the Sky,* Sandburg's *Chicago Poems,* and Frost's *Mountain Interval* simultaneously with Masters's *The Great Valley.* The year 1917 saw William Carlos Williams's *Book of Poems, Al Que Quiere!* and T. S. Eliot's *Prufrock and Other Observations.* The competition and the followers were making themselves heard. No wonder Masters at about this time in Chicago (possibly as early as 1915), sitting unseen behind a curtain, listened in a kind of terror as Powys extolled him as the direct descendant of Walt Whitman and of Chaucer, and made him feel that a burden of literary expectations had been placed upon him which he "could not carry."[4]

Nevertheless, by 1919 he had published not only the expanded "definitive" edition of the *Anthology,* but *Songs and Satires,* and a two-volume contribution to a Midwestern epic, *The Great Valley* (1916) and *Toward the Gulf* (1918). Like their successors, they develop a unity of theme principally in the water imagery of their titles. The successors are *Starved Rock* (1919)—named for "Le Rocher," a fortress on the river—, *The Open Sea* (1921), and "The New Atlantis," published as *The New World* in 1937. Some of the poems of each develop the history of the area and its people. The last in particular is a sustained and unified historical narrative of America from pre-Columbian discoveries to the 1930s. But it lacks a protagonist and dramatic intensity, and it is unified chiefly by Masters's anger at the greed for gold. It was his last attempt at a long narrative poem. The four others are collections of poems, some of regional history, some lyrics, some character descriptions (more elaborate versions of the *Spoon River* genre), with a certain amount of political, social, and religious satire, often with a scientific or psychological emphasis. Especially in the lyrics, but in many other poems as well, the reader who knows Masters's autobiography will be on familiar ground. In fact this autobiographical thread can add a certain interest to otherwise unprepossessing volumes.

Lois Teal Hartley, one of the more sympathetic as well as the most scholarly of early students of Masters, writes of *Toward the Gulf,* probably the best volume in the series: "Although the language is frequently rhetorical, turgid, overly analytical, and verbose, there are notable phrases and passages, as well as shrewd character studies. The prolixity causes many of the poems to lack pungency and incisiveness, and the intellectual longer poems sometimes become slightly obscure. Yet. . . ."[5] The scholarly objectivity indicated by Hartley's "Yet" and "Although" is commendable, but she does not persuade us, or attempt to, that this is successful or enjoyable poetry. Even the student of poetry—unless he is a specialist in Edgar Lee Masters—will not be tempted to sift these volumes for their occasional "notable phrases and passages."

Harriet Monroe, whose reviews in *Poetry* were a major source of support for Masters over the years, was more indulgent. She consistently emphasized "the poet's rich and generous personality," his "tremendous vitality," his "large canvas," his "range and power," his "heroic outlook." But she was obliged also to note his prosiness, his excessive "expansiveness," his undisciplined, "haphazard" arrangement of his materials. Denying that Masters was "a man of one book, who began and ended with *Spoon River,*" she nevertheless acknowledged that "Masters's Spoon River outburst was a tangent from his circle rather than part of its curve." And she celebrated his return to that tangent in the two books which were closest to *Spoon River—The New Spoon River* (1924) and *Lichee Nuts* (1930)—since "the Spoon River form of brevities suits Mr. Masters best by checking his expansiveness."[6] Indeed the reader will find incisive portraits and anecdotes in both of these books, the one a return to Spoon River a generation later, the other a collection of humorous and sympathetic portraits of Chinese Americans whom Masters had known in Chicago and New York. Yet neither approaches the unity and overall effect of the first *Spoon River.*

The year after *The New Spoon River* Masters published his *Selected Poems* (1925). The volume ends with twenty poems from *Spoon River* and eighteen from *The New Spoon River,* but nearly 400 preceding pages offer poems largely in conventional metrics with a wide range of mood and subject, grouped under such headings as "Dramatic

Portraits," "Stories in Verse," "Lyrics and Sonnets," "Dithyrambs," "Poems of Reflection." Again the new directions are a return to the arc of his curve in the older traditions of poetry. Monroe's defense of Masters's apostasy from vers libre is characteristic: "But his use of a loose blank verse and various rhymed measures, even for modern subjects, often justifies itself, not by delicacy and exactness, but by a rush and rigor which carry imperfections as a torrent carries drift and scum."[7]

In 1933 came a small volume, *The Serpent in the Wilderness.* Its principal piece, "Beethoven's Ninth Symphony and the King Cobra," is a long prose-poem which may owe something—in subject, metrics, and point of view—to D. H. Lawrence's poem "The Snake," published a decade earlier. A number of critics found it an impressive treatment of the problem of evil, symbolized by the monism of the cobra as opposed to the dualism of man.[8] It narrates the responses of a caged cobra to the music of Beethoven played on the radio. Like the majority of Masters's poetry after *Spoon River* and like many of the later, added *Spoon River* poems, the set of poems in *The Serpent in the Wilderness* might be called opinion-poems or idea-poems, presenting rather direct conclusions from the poet's thought, such as his faith in science, his hatred of the Judaeo-Christian ethic as opposed to the Greek, his paradoxical love of nature and attraction to the city, his consciousness of evil, usually symbolized by the venomous snake. *Invisible Landscapes* (1935) continues these preoccupations, particularly nature-worship, including nostalgic reminiscences of Masters's childhood—"New Salem Hill," "Concord Church," "Sandridge," "The Old Farm." Here again the central poem is "Beethoven's Ninth Symphony and the King Cobra."

In *Poems of People* (1936), published the same year as *Across Spoon River,* and in *More People,* which followed three years later, Masters returned to the portrait genre of *Spoon River.* In about one fifth of the poems in *More People,* he returned even to *Spoon River* events and persons ("Bill Dill" reveals the village idiot called "William Metcalf" in *Spoon River,* and known finally as Bill McNamar in *The Sangamon* [1942]). Two poems in *More People* have an odd, oblique interest. One, "Anson Harms," could be mistaken in its title, tone, and diction for one of E. A. Robinson's early Tilbury Town portraits. The other, "Confucius and Tsze-Lû," is a philosophical narrative dialogue presenting the conflicting attractions of Confucius and Lao-Tzu (Lao-Tse) and therefore something of the effect of Eastern thought on Masters, a subject that has been little studied. One indication of its importance is Eunice Tietjens's remark in *The World at My Shoulder* that sometime around 1916 or 1917 Masters "gave me a copy of the *Bhagavad-gita* and so changed the whole course of my spiritual existence."[9] Masters's last two books of poems, *Illinois Poems* (1914) and *Along the Illinois* (1942), were published, as Masters says in a prefatory note to *Illinois Poems,* "only a few miles from Spoon River." In content, too, they return to Petersburg and the Illinois background. All the *Illinois Poems* are rhymed.

At his death Masters left hundreds of uncollected poems (there is no edition of his collected poems), some published only in fugitive periodicals, many unpublished. Among these are "vignettes from Vermont," a series of brief, free-verse portraits of Vermonters in the *Spoon River* vein.[10] These are portraits of living persons, who speak of themselves to a visitor, without coming to any grand conclusions about "Life" or "Soul" such as mar many of the *Spoon River* portraits. Internal evidence, for example the comment of one character that his neighbor is buying up iron for the Japanese, indicates that they may have been written as late as 1943, the year Masters's health failed. If Masters had written or rewritten the *Spoon River* poems (and many others) in this maturer, more objective style, he might have continued to appeal much more successfully to the changing poetic tastes of this century.

Three Dramatic Tales

Domesday Book.   *Domesday Book* (1920) takes a different direction from these other post–*Spoon River* collections of poems. It is a long dramatic narrative, or rather a series of dramatic monologues, in blank verse telling a single story. Its origin is an unpublished story from Masters's Lewistown days concerning the differing accounts of witnesses to a suicide. In *Across Spoon River,* Masters felt constrained to give an account of its origin so as to make the point that he had written the story without ever having read any of Browning's *The Ring and the Book,* to which critics had compared *Domesday Book* (*ASR,* 369). A portion of that same early story was resurrected for the last novel, *The Tide of Time* (1937), in which the hero and his friends are witnesses to a suicide by a college mate.

But the existence of the story in manuscript,[11] the primary source, does not mean that Browning's *The Ring and the Book* was not a second major source for *Domesday Book*. Masters's acquaintance with Browning's poem dates at least from his paper, "Browning as a Philosopher," read before the Chicago Literary Club on 19 November 1912, and now in the Newberry Library, Chicago. A third source is mentioned at the close of *Across Spoon River*, where Masters describes the war fever of 1917 in Chicago. He mentions a certain attractive, sophisticated woman who, he heard, had left Chicago to enter a convent in France, undergoing as part of her initiation the chore of having to scrub floors.

The story centers on the death of Elenor Murray, whose body is discovered by a hunter on the shore of the Illinois River, much as a woman's body is discovered by Mitch Miller and his friend Skeeters in the novel *Mitch Miller*, also published in 1920. (In fact many such events recur in Masters's narratives, all of which have a large autobiographical element.) Elenor Murray, who shares Masters's initials, is, like him, a rebellious spirit determined not to be confined by narrow village moralities and prejudices. Her energy, intelligence, and will are recognizable qualities of heroines and heroes, including the hero of *Across Spoon River*. She has also qualities of Masters's emancipated lover, Tennessee Mitchell, as well as of his nurse Bertha Baum, down to the detail of oyster soup being fed to the recovering patient.[12] For a time during the war, Elenor Murray becomes a nun, scrubbing floors as part of her discipline.

The story emerges somewhat in the manner of the *Spoon River* narrative, insofar as it is a narrative of intertwined lives and events. The coroner, Merival, speaking for the author, decides to create his own "Domesday Book" through which he can reveal the nation's "tenures spiritual" (*DB*, 20), as King William's Domesday Book contained a tabulation of his kingdom's assets and resources, human and material. All those who can be found who knew Elenor testify in a series of monologues giving a composite picture of her life and of the American scene from about 1890 to 1920. The monologues are considerably longer than those of *Spoon River*, which gives them and the narrative a certain diffuseness never overcome by the single subject, the life and death of Elenor Murray. Actually, there is more than a single subject, since Elenor's story is intended, even by the coroner, to represent America's "tenures spiritual." "This Elenor Murray was America . . ." (*DB*, 354), says her lover Barrett Bays. At the conclusion, Merival's Aunt Cynthia proposes as symbol of

America the paragon "Arielle / And not your Elenor Murray" (*DB*, 371).

As it happens, two rather different critics commented on *Domesday Book* in contemporary reviews. One was Stuart Sherman, who had earlier indicated his distaste for *Spoon River Anthology*. He is the only negative critic mentioned by name in *Across Spoon River*. In his home state, Masters tells us, he was subjected to vicious personal criticism by a Professor Sherman (*ASR*, 370); Stuart Pratt Sherman is one of the sources of Masters's hatred and scorn for "professors." The second critic was Padraic Colum, a long-time friend of Masters whom he frequently visited in New York. Sherman in the *Yale Review* for April 1921 and Colum in the *New Republic* of 29 December 1920 both called attention to Elenor Murray's frantic searching from place to place, from lover to lover. Sherman emphasized Masters's belief that she was "seeking for peace," and Colum her "search for beauty" and its "effects . . . on those whose lives touched hers."[13] The two critics agree about Masters's telling insight into the lives he portrayed—that his characters were frustrated chiefly by their own willfulness. It was not so much external forces such as poverty, lack of educational opportunity, village morality, unsympathetic family and associates, the acquisitiveness and selfishness of others, or even the sex drive or fate that caused this futile searching. It was their own lack of discipline.

This interesting consensus by two generally opposed critics may, by extension, serve as an hypothesis from which to examine Masters's search for the continuing arc of his circle, different from the tangent of *Spoon River*. The characters Masters presents as heroes or heroines of all his narratives, poetic and fictional and dramatic, are in many ways typically American and quite believable. They are usually first presented, like the archetypal Huck Finn, as oppressed by circumstance and by the avarice, hypocrisy, ill will of others. All of them struggle to break out, to find their own "beauty" or "peace" through self-expression. Some of them find a tentative or transient satisfaction, usually in premarital or extramarital love. Somewhat in contrast to the few saved souls in *Spoon River*, almost none of the characters of Masters's fiction achieve fulfillment. Most of them, particularly the protagonists, seem to seek sensation rather than peace or beauty, and they indeed find it. But, and here we are closer to *Spoon River* again, only the pioneers and those who follow the old life-style find true fulfillment. It is as though order and discipline had disappeared from American life with the generation of pioneers, and even Masters, who acutely felt the loss of these fundamental values, could not recapture them. In *Domesday Book,* and in its sequel, *The Fate of the Jury,* there are none of these pioneers.

Fate of the Jury. *The Fate of the Jury* (1929) is one of Masters's many epilogues. One might say even that he had a weakness for the epilogue—a concluding section intended to round out the design and clarify the meaning of the work. Hence the blank verse mock-heroic "Spooniad," which concluded the first edition of *Spoon River* in 1915, and the second afterthought, actually entitled "Epilogue," added to the definitive edition of 1916. Hence *The Fate of the Jury,* which follows the lives of the coroner's jury which had meticulously examined the life and death of Elenor Murray and the "riffles," or impingements, of her life on others. Seven of those others are now seen to be the jurors themselves and the coroner Merival, whom her death has brought together.

Of the six jurors, two are worth mention because of their un-mistakable modeling on men formerly important in Masters's life. One is the pessimist David Barrow, a not-too invidious portrait of Masters's former law partner Clarence Darrow. The other is the editor Winthrop Marion, a portrait of William Marion Reedy. The biographical material Masters included from Reedy's life is extensive and detailed and even a bit sensational. The plot of the book is to have each jury member reveal, before his death, the controlling secret of his life—a continuation of the confessional character of *Domesday Book* and of *Spoon River.* Not all the jurors finally reveal themselves, but Winthrop Marion confesses and gains stature as he does so. Much of the information is corroborated in Masters's article on Reedy, "Literary Boss of the Middle West," published in the *American Mercury* for April 1935, six years after publication of *Fate of the Jury.* The more sensational aspects are Marion's (Reedy's) having used his newspaper to extort money from those who feared publicity, using the money for joys of the flesh: "I sold myself," he confesses sadly (147); and his financial dependence on and final marriage to the mistress of a "sporting house" (148). His friend the coroner Merival, hero of the story, is present at his death and observes the beauty of his "dead face, now so crystalline" (143), much as Masters, present for Reedy's funeral, meditated upon the face of his dead friend.

The similarity of Masters and Merival returns us to a second plot of *Fate of the Jury*, the love affair between Merival and Arielle, the beautiful, talented woman introduced at the close of *Domesday Book* as an alternate symbol of America. Of all the characters in both books, Merival comes closest to achieving beauty and peace. He marries Arielle, but her beauty and the beauty of their marriage is flawed by a strain of insanity in her family, which precludes children and which soon asserts itself in Arielle. Merival lives on to a wise and unembittered and finally peaceful old age.

Like nearly all of Masters's other books, including *Spoon River*, *Fate of the Jury* gains a great deal of interest from the reader's knowledge of Masters's biography. We recognize Masters's Petersburg boyhood in Merival's recollection of "flying kites in April" (5). We note the great difference in age between Merival and Arielle—his graying temples, her "sunny hair" (19)—and recall Masters's marriage to Ellen Coyne, thirty years his junior, in 1926, three years before *Fate of the Jury* was published in 1929; and that Merival had "lost / A woman twenty years before" (13), paralleling Masters's tumultuous, brief affair with Tennessee Mitchell which had begun in 1909.

Finally we note an odd, even far-fetched, connection between Masters's biography and Merival's sense of the symbolism of "Boy, the dog, / The Airedale" (2–3) that had sought him out and loved him. Merival wonders "If somehow Boy was symbol . . . / Of Arielle" (4), who had also sought him—which establishes something more than an alphabetical connection between "Arielle" and "Airedale." On the biographical side, Hardin Masters relates that Masters as a child "had a black dog . . . the size of an airedale" called Hohne Boy, "and all other dogs we had as a family he insisted on calling by the same name."[14] Further, we observe that in 1928 a boy was born to Ellen Coyne Masters. The father quite naturally was proud and hopeful. Masters had not yet seen the boy, born in Kansas City, the home of Ellen Masters's parents. But a month earlier he had written a sonnet to his son Hilary, who was, he said, as his youngest child more immediately related to him than was any other person.[15] A direct connection between the childless Merival's dog Boy and Masters's son Hilary, his only child with his second wife, is on the surface ridiculous. Yet symbolic meanings seldom lie on the surface. He may have had fears, which other strands in *Fate of the Jury* corroborate, that the physical separation from his second wife would expand (as it later did), and that he should lose this boy.

One strand in the melodramatic plot of *Fate of the Jury* involves two women friends of Arielle with whom she is as intimate as Elenor Murray of *Domesday Book* had been as a schoolgirl with Alma Bell, a teacher who was persecuted by the town for what they assumed was a perverted affection for the girl. After the marriage of Arielle and Merival, one of these friends comes to Arielle in poverty, and Arielle, the madness coming on her, attacks the woman with a knife. The servants subdue her, but not before she has killed Merival's much loved dog, Boy. Another strand in the melodrama involves Merival's secret trip, before the marriage, to Arielle's childhood home to check on details of her life which she has given him. In a third strand, the banker, Ritter, confesses that his secret sorrow results from the lesbian affections of his wife, which he discovers by reading her personal letters. This wife, after their son's birth, "slept alone" (99) and repulsed poor Ritter. Finally Ritter loses his wife, his fortune, and his only son.

Ritter's situation is close to that of Masters at the time of his divorce in 1923. There is the additional resemblance of the wife Margaret Ritter to Tennessee Mitchell, if one substitutes for the female lover Georgine the unnamed male lover of "Deirdre" described in *Across Spoon River*. Furthermore, Masters seems to have accepted, or perhaps wished to justify, spying by a man on his wife or lover. The autobiographical hero of *Skeeters Kirby* sets a detective to spy on his wife Alicia, and later himself hides ignominiously under her bed in an attempt to trap her. Kirby's basis for divorce, revealed by the spying, is the operation, prior to their marriage, which made it impossible for Alicia to bear children. Parenthetically, we can observe here that Alicia's later setting a detective to spy upon him in the sequel, *Mirage,* is quite another story.

Intrinsically *The Fate of the Jury* has less to recommend it to the nonspecialist reader than *Domesday Book*. As a coda to the earlier work, it cannot quite stand alone. The blank verse is sustained but regular in tone: all the characters speak with the voice of Edgar Lee Masters, and act out much of his biography as well. Extrinsically, to the specialist in Masters, *Fate of the Jury* may prove one of the more fascinating of his works, precisely because there is so much of that authorial voice revealing itself behind the seven principal male characters. Two brief additions to those already cited may be mentioned here. The Reverend Maiworm, the least notable of the jurors, confesses that his life was blighted by an alliance against him of his mother and sister, an affliction of which Masters complains in describing his childhood years in *Across Spoon River*. Again, Winthrop Marion (Reedy) defines the poet, declaring that he must "bring no regret, no self-contempt, no hate" (143) to his verse, and that "loss of faith / In self" (144) and "contempt / For women" (147) resulting from excessive "faring free" are inimical to poetry. The fascination lies in the confessions of the author behind the confessions of his characters. All of the qualities which Reedy, the one trustworthy critic, here cites as inimical to poetry are observable explicitly or implicitly in Masters's self-portrait in *Across Spoon River*.

The Golden Fleece of California. Before proceeding to Masters's prose fiction, we can afford brief mention here to a third book-length narrative poem, *The Golden Fleece of California* (1936). Part autobiography, part fiction, part allegory, part epic, it is an ambitious attempt, in iambic pentameter verse, to transpose the Greek epic to America. The narrator hero resembles Masters in his absorption in Greek (at McKendree College instead of Knox College—both in Illinois), his "reading Homer in the Spring" (10), his pursuit of wealth symbolized by his courting a rich widow (an event which recurs in much of Masters's fiction, evidently based on his courtship of Lillian P. Wilson in 1921), and his patriotism. Five youths travel to California with a girl, Arete, the wife of one of them. Arete's husband is drowned in the Platte River (as was an uncle of Masters whom he never knew). Finally only the narrator and one friend survive. The friend has found peace in carpentry and growing apple trees; the narrator, like America, is still enmeshed in "strands of The Golden Fleece" (74)—the dream of wealth.

Masters's attempt to capitalize on the perennial interest in the California Gold Rush succeeded no better than the search of his characters. The narrative plods, and the verse alternates between pretentiousness and triviality. Masters shows a sincere interest in American history and appreciation of the irony of his mythological analogue. Yet the ideas are never translated successfully into dramatic action, and the end effect is heavy-handed moralism.

Chapter Eight
Spoon River into Fiction
Memories of Boyhood

Many readers have described or at least thought of *Spoon River Anthology* as a novel in verse. Doubtless the occasional reader of *Domesday Book* or *Fate of the Jury* has thought the same. Masters insisted in *Across Spoon River* and "The Genesis of Spoon River" and elsewhere that what eventually became *Spoon River* was originally intended as a novel, which was to be his only book. In "The Genesis of Spoon River" he speaks of his early interest in becoming a short story writer and of his early attempts at fiction, much influenced by Edgar Allan Poe (44). In 1920, the same year as *Domesday Book*, he published his first novel, *Mitch Miller*. It was the first of five published in the five years between 1920 and 1925, written one a year (besides three books of poetry)—one, *Skeeters Kirby*, even rewritten from memory after the manuscript was lost on Masters's return from Europe in 1921. These novels, as well as the later *Kit O'Brien* (1927) and *The Tide of Time* (1937), are related in terms of locale, characters, events, theme, and time.

Mitch Miller.   As a prose novel *Mitch Miller* (1920) is superficially altogether different from *Spoon River*. But as a reminiscence of Masters's childhood in the Petersburg area with a reintroduction to certain familiar characters, it is very much in the *Spoon River* line. It is also, as already mentioned, very much in the *Tom Sawyer* line, and is, in fact, not a bad imitation or pastiche of Mark Twain's famous book for boys. Skeeters Kirby as narrator and "chum" of Mitch is clearly Masters as he portrayed himself in *Across Spoon River* and elsewhere, except where Masters is also Mitch, precociously in love with Zueline, and an avid reader and thinker. Any reader of the autobiography or of *Spoon River* can trace here familiar events and characters. And anyone familiar with *Tom Sawyer* can enjoy the interrelationships of the two boys trying to emulate Tom and Huck, who were the alter egos of Mark Twain, while Masters, who was both of them (or all four: Skeeters playing Huck and Mitch playing Tom), tries to surpass his own model, Mark Twain.

As in *Tom Sawyer*, much of the plot concerns the boys' search for buried treasure. Early in the book they find it, only to have it quickly confiscated by adult authority in the person of Skeeters's father, the attorney Hardy Kirby (who is close to Masters's father Hardin or "Hardy" Masters). The father lectures them somewhat sententiously, pointing out the "lesson" that every childhood pain recurs "when you grow up, only on a bigger scale, and hurts more" (44). Much later, the boys' fathers take them on a trip to fulfill their hearts' desire—a visit to the real Tom Sawyer. He turns out to be only a butcher of the same name. The boys are disillusioned and heartsick. Reverend Miller, Mitch's father, tries to comfort his son in almost the same words lawyer Kirby had used, saying, in Mitch's rendering, "that everything that happens when you're a boy, happens over when you're a man, just like it, but hurts worse. And that people must dis-ci-pline themselves to stand it, and make the most of life, and do for others, and love God and keep his commandments" (210–11). The best lines in the book are Mitch's final comment on this episode, "And then Mitch said: 'I'm mad at my pa. He ought not to brought me here. . . . He ought to have left us still believin' in the book' " (211).

The unstated ironies of the failure of the minister father ignorantly destroying the faith of his son, and the greater wisdom of the son wishing he could still believe in the good book *(Tom Sawyer)* he has lived by, are touchingly presented in rare understatement. As usual, however, Masters does not quite trust his readers and so adds an epilogue in his own voice. He had told the story fairly and convincingly in the country dialect of his midwestern boyhood; the boys occasionally fail to drop a final *g*, yet it is a remarkably consistent performance. But the epilogue, characteristically, is out of key with the rest of the book. For the reader it is like the experience of the boys' discovering that there is no real Tom Sawyer. The illusion of reality vanishes and the book turns into a tract. Masters, remembering Mitch's torture at losing Zueline, says that it is as well that Mitch Miller died at age twelve, after being run over while hitching rides on a train. If he had lived, "over and over again, perhaps, he might have poured out his passion in the endless search for beauty and faith, and in the search for realization . . . and . . .

he would have never found them, through woman" (261). He does
not mention that Mitch's torture was really Masters's own, and that
his own futile search was continuing. He concludes with an odd
diatribe against "treasure hunters" (262–63), a reiterated phrase.
"Treasure hunters" have brought about all the failures, the loss of
freedoms in America since the Civil War. Mitch has been spared
these further disillusionments, but the author has not been spared.

The epilogue undercuts nearly everything the novel seemed to
stand for. The illusion of the boys' story is lost, and with it the
idea of the importance of illusion as a sustaining force. The concept
of the boys' treasure hunting as an enterprise valid in itself—a
quest—is destroyed by Masters's deprecatory use of the term "treasure hunters." The satire on the platitudes of adult rationalizations
is undercut by Masters's adoption of adult morality at the end, and
his assertion that in adult life the failures and disappointments of
childhood really are repeated, but hurt worse. And the implied
satire on Christian hypocrisy dissolves in the author's corroboration
of the message of Mitch's funeral sermon, which was that "if it
hadn't been for the best, Mitch wouldn't have died; and that God
knew best and we didn't; and if we could look ahead and see the
dreadful things that would happen, we'd know that God was good
and wise to take Mitch away before they happened" (253). Like
Johnnie Sayre in the *Spoon River* epitaph, he is saved "from the evil
to come"—which again would be ironic except that Johnnie (Mitch)
is made to say that someone was "wise to chisel for me" those very
words.

Kit O'Brien, another epilogue.   Immediately related to *Mitch
Miller* is its sequel *Skeeters Kirby* (1923) and a third novel *Mirage*
(1924), forming a trilogy. Somewhat later appeared the novel *Kit
O'Brien* (1927), which is tangential to the Skeeters Kirby trilogy.
It can be dealt with briefly here as a second epilogue or afterthought
to *Mitch Miller*. Kit is a member of a gang that fights with Mitch
and Skeeters in the earlier book in order to avenge a thrashing of
Kit by Mitch (38). *Kit O'Brien*, like *Mitch Miller*, is set in Petersburg,
but the Petersburg of the second book is much more nearly Spoon
River than the village where Mitch and Skeet lived and played. In
fact Masters felt called upon to add a prefatory note explaining that
criticisms of the town were meant to apply "to the American small
town in general," and not to his beloved childhood home. It is
Spoon River also in some of its characters and its melodrama. Here

Aba Sprinkle, the villainous state's attorney, is opposed by Hardy
Kirby for the forces of righteousness. Kirby continues to represent
Edgar Lee's father Hardin Masters. The melodrama includes Kit's
hiding in a houseboat on the Mississippi with an ex-actor who is a
religious fanatic and an ex-actress who has lost her beauty, and his
rescue of the actress at peril of being arrested (for having stolen a
pie). As in *Mitch Miller*, the story is told in the first-person boyish
dialect of a participant, this time Kit.

At the start, Mitch is referred to as having beaten Kit in their
fight by unfair means, using "knucks" (2, 24). This makes the idol
and "chum" of Skeeters Kirby and the hero of *Mitch Miller* into a
cheat, or it makes the hero of *Kit O'Brien* into a liar. There seems
no way out of the dilemma. To establish a second connection with
Mitch Miller Masters is forced to revise his account of the accident
which caused Mitch's death. It now seems that instead of accidentally
falling under the train, Mitch had been knocked off the train by a
guard. The two boys who had been with him are said to know of
the real cause, and therefore the corrupt district attorney, conniving
with the railroad lawyers, has the boys imprisoned for stealing a
pie. Kit had participated in the pie stealing, but had not been
caught. Masters himself cannot decide whether or when Kit knew
about the train guard's implication in the death of Mitch. The first
mention of it occurs when Kit is hiding outside a window and hears
George Montgomery (a good samaritan who makes a home for various unjustly persecuted souls) tell how Mitch was killed: "Then
George went on to tell a story that I knowed nothin' about and
which knocked me cold, which was about Mitch Miller" (13). He
is still hiding, as he has been for many weeks, from the authorities
who have arrested the other two boys, and now sees his predicament
in a new light. "Well, wouldn't they want me out of the way too,
thinkin' I knowed about Mitch?" (14). Within ten pages, he is
telling his story to George, who has taken him in; and he includes,
in his explanation of his motivation for running away, the account
he has heard from George himself, and for the first time, the night
before. This time he appears inexplicably to be lying to his benefactor
George, or to the reader.

Other flaws include a much less consistent use of boyish idiom,
with many slips into adult or educated pronunciations and vocab-
ulary, and further discrepancies in plot—such as how the ex-actress,
Miss Siddons, lost her beauty, whether by disease or by injecting

wax under the skin to remove wrinkles. The tale's familiar themes are the oppressive hypocrisy of the small town, fomented by preachers and newspaper editors and perpetrated by corrupt lawyers and judges, and the socially ineffective but individually saving benevolence of a small group of enlightened spirits. It is an unimpressive performance, best written off as a potboiler, a source of immediate income, such as most writers have been obliged to produce once they have felt committed to making their livings by their pens.

Memories of Manhood

Skeeters Kirby, a sequel. Masters wrote *Skeeters Kirby* (1923) immediately after *Mitch Miller*, probably much of it on shipboard during his trip to Europe in the summer of 1921. But when the manuscript was lost or stolen on his return to America, he was forced to rewrite it, so it appeared after *Children of the Market Place* (1922). But *Skeeters* is a true sequel to *Mitch Miller*. The first fifty pages are written in the same dialect that Skeeters used to tell Mitch's story. This is a bit illogical, since Skeeters is telling of his high school years and writing in the past tense, presumably from the age of thirty-three, at the end of the book. Still, it is an acceptable convention, and it is dropped at the moment of meeting Winifred Hervey—Ann in *Across Spoon River*, Margaret George in real life— evidently the moment which for Masters separates the young man from his childhood. Of all the novels, *Skeeters Kirby* has the most precise and easily identifiable parallels in the autobiography.

Masters makes no bones about the fact that his fiction is autobiographical, so it is not surprising that Masters had little difficulty rewriting *Skeeters Kirby* after losing the manuscript. Unfortunately, it is interesting only as an account of Masters's life. As a novel it is poorly plotted, unconvincing, prolix, and diffuse. Even the hero Kirby, though he is the one moderately convincing character, is uninteresting and quite unprepossessing. He is oddly like the hero of *Across Spoon River* in this respect. The protagonist in each pictures himself in all ingenuousness as a self-indulgent, self-pitying opportunist ready to exploit others, particularly women.

This candor is admirable but at first baffling. Why should Masters be willing to present such an unflattering picture of himself, which must have turned numerous readers away from these books, and scholars from the study of his canon? The obvious answer may be the correct one: that it never occurred to him that he was presenting an unflattering self-portrait; it was merely an honest one. If it was honest and accurate, Masters had sufficient confidence in his energy and charm—his charisma—to feel certain it would win him new admirers. He seems never to have been lacking in admirers and friends, both male and female, willing to sacrifice their own interests for his. It is a legitimate philosophical or at least semantic question whether exploitation of those willing and even anxious to be exploited is still exploitation.

The first friend and lover willing to be exploited in *Skeeters Kirby* is Winifred Hervey. Skeeters rightly considers her his superior. She has read more, thought more, and written more and better than he. She becomes his instructor in literature and in love. "Winifred was my joy and companion. She had really taken the place of Mitch. I had found a friend at last. She had brought me into her room of books" (57). Later he tells her he has " 'always grieved for lost days, departed happiness, changes, separations: and now, Winifred, you take the place of all of it. You sum up all that I ever felt in going away from the farm, in leaving my grandmother, in parting with Mitch' " (104). Altogether Skeeters Kirby is much more sincere, subservient, and wooing than Masters makes himself out to be in his relations with Ann in *Across Spoon River*.

In the next section of the novel, George Higgins—Maltravers in *Across Spoon River*, Ernest McGaffey in real life—is Skeet's confidant and supporter. Meanwhile, there is Julie Valentine, who is kind to him while he is ill. He finds he is aroused, possibly by "her maternal" qualities (184). (She is portrayed in *Across Spoon River* simply as Julia, who bestowed on him "maternal caresses," and told him he needed a woman to care for him and to see that his laundry was done [*ASR,* 207]. This Julia advised Masters to marry Stella, another girl friend, since Julia, like Julie, is already married and the mistress of a gambler.)

Kirby's friend Roger gives him similar practical advice, " 'You'll be getting married one of these days; and why not marry to advantage and not to disadvantage?' " (216). He proposes Martha Fisk, daughter of a multimillionaire who is dying of diabetes. Kirby sets his net for Martha and begins to see her. In the meantime, he becomes involved with the captivating Alicia Adams. At this stage Alicia is Tennessee Mitchell; and Martha Fisk, homely but rich, is "the Golden Aura" as Masters calls the only daughter of the president of a railroad, later his wife in *Across Spoon River*, in real life Helen Jenkins. In the autobiography the pill Masters must swallow to obtain entrée to Chicago society and to rise as a lawyer is sugar-coated. The president of the railroad is not so rich as he had been, but his daughter is beautiful and physically attractive. In *Skeeters Kirby*, Kirby is willing to take the homely girl (throughout their engagement enjoying the charms of Alicia), but the millionaire father finally breaks the engagement. Kirby immediately takes the ring Martha has returned and gives it to Alicia, and they are married.

Through fiction Masters is able to experience a sort of vicarious marriage with Tennessee Mitchell, whom he would have married about 1910 if his wife had been willing to release him. The marriage of Kirby and Alicia is not very successful. Kirby wants to have children; Alicia does not—in fact cannot, as Kirby's spying eventually reveals, because of an operation she has withheld from him. He temporizes, seeking advice from friends who had known him in earlier times. One of these is "Grinner" Newton, a friend from high school days in Marshalltown (Masters's name here for Lewistown, derived from his hatred for Justice Marshall, whose Hamiltonian philosophy Masters felt had led America to the Civil War and destruction). Grinner had been sent to college by the church when Kirby was forced to study law while his sister went to college in his stead. Grinner has gone on with the help of his church to become a doctor of philosophy and of laws, to acquire the education that Masters all his life wished he might have had. But Grinner has become an oleaginous sycophant and hypocrite, "For in truth he is not 'Grinner' Newton any more" (300). The owner of that nickname in Lewistown high school had been Edgar Lee "Grinner" Masters.

After the death of his sainted grandmother, Kirby journeys to the funeral in Petersburg, which retains its proper name throughout the trilogy. Afterward he is "intense and set of will. I would be rid of Alicia" (307). From this point on—not earlier, despite the marriage—Alicia is modeled on Helen Jenkins Masters, and Kirby, having walked out of her life, soon begins a new relationship with Becky Norris. Kirby plays Tom Sawyer to her Becky Thatcher as they create a few idyllic moments in a natural setting on a river where Kirby is writing poems and recovering himself after the break with Alicia. The poems, written under a pseudonym, soon create a stir, as his friend Bob Hayden (William Marion Reedy) keeps him informed. The affair with Becky progresses. Masters gives her some of the melodramatic background of Tennessee Mitchell—a drunken father beating her and driving her from home, her fleeing to the house of an aunt and then to Chicago, still in her teens. But essentially she is the mysterious Pamela, mentioned only once near the end of *Across Spoon River* as the "magic princess" who would make every thing right and beautiful (405).

Kirby is wary of Becky and leaves for Chicago and New York, to see the publishers who are about to issue his book of poems, which have been causing a sensation—like the *Spoon River Anthology*—in the serial press. As he leaves he says, "And all of Becky receded from me like a dream" (350). In Chicago his friend George Higgins, whose cabin he had borrowed near Becky's more palatial home, tells him practically that he should pursue Becky and marry her, that she is a wealthy widow, and "What better use can these widows make of their money than to give leisure to men of talent?" (352).

Kirby immediately writes to her, " 'Becky Darling: I have thought of nothing but you since I left you.' " He signs the letter, " 'Tom' " (353). Soon he is divorced, at great expense to himself, since his enemy Cavette Errant (Clarence Darrow), who has become Alicia's lawyer, has gouged the last penny from him. He asks Becky to marry him, but she will not. The book ends with some philosophizing by Bob Hayden (Reedy), while Kirby, lonely and depressed, has visions of the departed Becky. The date is 1911, Kirby is thirty-three. His book which he gives to Becky is both Masters's *Songs and Sonnets* (1910), which appeared during his affair with Tennessee, and *Spoon River*; and it is also *Domesday Book* (1920), which appeared the year Masters finally gave up his law office in Chicago and while he was engaged in bitter divorce proceedings with Mrs. Masters.

Mirage.   *Mirage* (1924), which appeared the year after *Skeeters Kirby*, begins as a perfect sequel, with Becky receiving Kirby's letter in answer to hers rejecting him. Soon discrepancies enter. *Mirage* is written in the third person, told no longer by Kirby but by the omniscient author. As Becky muses on Kirby's letter she admits, "He had made great sacrifices for her, to protect her name" (16). Gradually we learn that Kirby surrendered his fortune to his wife Alicia, not simply to be free of her as in *Skeeters Kirby*, but because she and her lawyer Cavette Errant (Darrow) had put detectives on him (tit for tat) and found out about Becky and her wealth and threatened to expose Becky: extortion. And Kirby had been obliged to protect her name. Another minor discrepancy occurs early in the story when Kirby meets in Chicago the detective he had sent to spy upon Alicia. The detective's name has oddly changed from Tom Murray in *Skeeters Kirby* to Tom Megary, probably simply because Masters misremembered it and as usual did not bother to check. As the story progresses the book Kirby has written becomes merely an early book of poetry, and his true literary success, the analogue of Masters's *Spoon River* success, occurs near the end of the novel.

Then there are internal discrepancies. In a long confession to Bob Hayden (who is still Reedy) of the details of his divorce and his relationship with Becky, Kirby insists that he never told Becky anything about the sordid extortion (137), yet in the first chapter the omniscient author has her musing about Kirby's "great sacrifices . . . to protect her name." Also Masters has her recollect a conversation in which she tells Kirby she will taunt an earlier lover with the advice that she has "met a real man at last," meaning Kirby, at which Kirby warns her that that might " 'give opportunity for a masculine retaliation' " (10–11). During his confession to Hayden, Kirby repeats this fear, and says, " 'I could think these things, but I could not say them [to Becky]' " (130). Why would he lie about these details to his best friend from whom he is seeking advice and help? How should he be so precise or so sure if he had forgotten? If he has forgotten, or is lying, what point is Masters making about that fact? Evidently none.

Masters's difficulty is that he is not creating characters and events and letting them work out their own interactions and consequences. He is *remembering* characters and events; and he has understandable difficulty distinguishing one remembering of a given event from another remembering of the same event. A second difficulty is that he is intentionally mixing up his memories to create his purported fiction. For example, the conversation with Reedy about the alleged extortion attempt by Darrow could never have taken place. Reedy died in 1920, his death accurately portrayed toward the end of this novel (413). Masters's divorce problems, complicated by his love for Lillian P. Wilson, came to a head in April 1921, and continued until the final decree of 1923. Also known as Mrs. J. Wood Wilson, Lillian was evidently a wealthy widow whom Masters expected to marry if he could expedite his divorce. Some 600 letters from her to Masters have been cataloged in the Hilary Masters Collection at Brown University. Doubtless they were all answered, or they were themselves answers, for Masters was an indefatigable letter writer. As we become aware of the tremendous volume of his correspondence, and recognize that Masters was nearly continuously writing— letters, books, poems—about the same events, we cease to wonder that he sometimes confused the uses he had made of his memories.

Although the novel *Mirage* is full of such details, only one or two need detain us further. Becky's relationship with Kirby, like Winifred's and Julia's, has a significant maternal element. Kirby visits Becky against his friend Hayden's advice and his own scruples, and observes how attractive she is, "soft and flaming with desire," and how closely she resembles his mother. Shelley's line occurs to him, "Would we were born of the same mother!" as he wishes to be of one blood with his lover—"that strange joy in an incestuous passion" (157). Slightly later in the same interview he again observes to himself Becky's resemblance to his mother (161). Finally, Becky "smiled her delight" and repeats, " 'Kiss mother' " (162).

In *Mirage* Kirby discovers a strong attachment for his actual mother, who has become a wealthy woman through some inheritance and oil interests. In the latter part of the novel she buys a large country place in Great Neck, Long Island, on the water and puts her lawyer son in charge of her affairs. It is Masters's one fully sympathetic treatment of his mother. Masters may have drawn this portrait in reaction or recrimination from the bitter, vindictive picture of her in *The Nuptial Flight* (1923) published the preceding year. The title *Mirage* refers to the vain pursuit of the image of the beautiful woman who will bring happiness—ostensibly Becky. When Kirby's mother returns to New York from Europe, Kirby already knows he has lost Becky. He hopes his mother has come "to be . . . an understanding mother to him for the rest of his life. How he longed to love her fully . . . and bind himself to her more firmly" (288). As she gradually provides him indispensable financial and moral support, Kirby observes to himself, "What a wise friend she had become!" (258). She is even, like Kirby himself, prescient: when Kirby was thirty-eight she had said to him, "You will be yourself at 45. . . . Only go and strive" (403). Kirby stays and strives, with her support, and, like Masters, at forty-five writes the poems which become his greatest success.

Kirby's insights are more mystical than his mother's. At one point Becky is in a hospital and Kirby, depressed in a cheap hotel, drinks himself into oblivion. In his dream, "he had seen her face with wonderful vividness. She was stretching her hands to him and saying, 'I love you so, I love you so' . . ." (189). "And at this moment" Becky was under anesthetic, undergoing an operation, dreaming of Kirby, as her friend beside her heard her say " 'I love you so, I love you . . .' " (191). On another occasion he receives a letter from a woman friend. "For some instinctive reason he put it in his pocket, deferring its reading." He explains to his companion, " 'I sometimes know when a letter contains things I don't want to hear, even before I open them" (308–9). Finally he reads the letter. "True to his clairvoyance it contained evil tidings" (311).

Kirby's companion on this occasion is Charlotte, formerly his secretary in Chicago, whom he had turned to in his loneliness after a second rupture with Becky. He recalls "her skill in serving him . . . in a word how devoted she was to his interests, not for the hire, but because she wanted to see him prosper in his work" (230–31). He obtains her a position as his mother's secretary, and he contentedly accepts her ministrations offered with "the tenderness of a mother and the fidelity of a servant" (315). These intimacies take place in his mother's home, where Charlotte worries about deceiving Mrs. Kirby, while Kirby insists there is no deception since his mother certainly knows and, he implies, tacitly approves. All the while he dreams of Becky and once indulges in a hallway flirtation with another woman, accidentally seen by Charlotte. Charlotte realizes she is merely an object for Kirby's exploitation and leaves. Finally she writes to Kirby, reminding him that she had lived with him "in every intimacy" and has been to him all "that a woman can be to a man," but that he had never admitted her to his life "in the slightest way" (391). He shows the letter to his mother, who tells him he is "cold and hard sometimes, selfish and cruel; and perhaps that makes an artist, but it makes it hard on the hearts that you really need for life" (392). Kirby listens in all humility and then attributes the difficulty to "this secret faculty of his soul which aroused demons in other people, this faculty which . . . had evoked the worst of Alicia. . . . And then Becky . . . and now Charlotte: Was he always to lose and eventually to be all alone in life, when his mother died or departed?" Tears come to his eyes in his terror at "life . . . prevised in this way" (393).

This is remarkably efficient rationalization, which turns one's guilt immediately into a "secret faculty" of the soul that brings out the worst in others—this worst that Kirby feels lies hidden and threatening, even in the innocent and devoted Charlotte. Kirby's prevision here, sentimental and self-pitying, is unremarkable. So is Masters's insight into his own nature. But his prevision in 1924 of his situation ten and more years in the future seems extraordinary. For he portrayed in Charlotte a woman who seems not to have entered his life until about 1936: Alice Davis, his devoted secretary during his years at the Hotel Chelsea from 1936 to 1943. Miss Davis, whom he called Anita, or, affectionately, Hen, in his customary way of revising the names of his women friends, was Masters's secretary, companion, housekeeper, mother, daughter, and friend. Evidently he at one time hoped to adopt her legally so as to be able to do more for her.[1]

In *Mirage* Charlotte dies of typhoid fever, which Kirby also contracts (from her), though he recovers quickly. In life, Masters became very ill in December 1943 and had to be hospitalized. At this point Mrs. Masters arrived to rescue him, after they had been separated for many years. Miss Davis retired into the background as a secretary no longer needed. Masters never fully recovered from his illness, but Mrs. Masters (his second wife) nursed him and cared for him for nearly seven years with the maternal devotion and solicitude for which he had searched all his life.

The Oedipal imagery in Masters's novels, particularly *Mirage,* is not necessarily evidence of repressed yearnings emerging symbolically from his subconscious. Masters read Freud—as nearly everything else of scientific, political, literary relevance—with interest and some thoroughness. What he found corroborated by his personal experience, his awareness, his feelings, he adopted or adapted into his own beliefs and attitudes, which he expressed in his writing. Throughout his description of the Petersburg-Lewistown years in *Across Spoon River,* he makes clear his dissatisfaction with his mother. Masters seems to have been hyperconscious of his own deprivations, particularly what he considered his childhood lack of maternal affection. Therefore he portrayed it as a controlling influence in life generally, as indeed it probably was in his own. It was a void that had somehow to be filled—by substitution, by reconciliation, or by reliving. Masters used all three approaches.

He never says or overtly suggests that his lifelong dedication to the pursuit of the "eternal feminine" was an attempt to fill this void from his childhood. Yet his autobiography indicates that it was so. His grandmother was his first and most important surrogate, so much so that he strove to emulate and even to be his grandfather: he insisted that when he was at his best he was his grandfather "reincarnated" (*ASR*, 403). Another early surrogate for his mother in the Petersburg years, when Masters was under twelve, was a Mrs. Moulton. Masters tells of his deep affection for her, to the degree that when she departed he "wept bitterly," to the annoyance of his mother (*ASR*, 46). Others were girls he was attracted to, according to his "precocious passion," from the age of six on. One of these, an older cousin, encouraged his advances, then told his mother, who punished him severely. Still others were Lucy and Zueline and Margaret George or "Anne" (*ASR*, 87 ff.).

Dorothy Dow knew Masters as well as anyone in a position and with the capacity to judge. She first met him about 1920, when he was pursuing "Pamela" (whom Miss Dow mentions by that name, making it clear that she was not herself Pamela, as some readers have surmised). He was then Miss Dow's suitor. About fifteen years later they met again in New York and became close friends. Miss Dow's "Edgar Lee Masters: An Introduction to Some Letters,"[2] is probably the best available account of his personality.[3] She tells of his inviting her to go with him to Europe as his secretary and of his mingling endearments with advice to take typing lessons the better to care for his manuscripts. She did not go to Europe with him and did not succumb to his blandishments (much to the annoyance of Dreiser, who told her any woman should be delighted to give herself to a great artist). She speaks of his essential romanticism, of his yearning to be loved and to have all the comfortable appurtenances of domesticity, while fancying himself in the role of Great Lover. Her summary of his long search for feminine perfection is one that any careful reader of *Across Spoon River* and the novels would have to agree with: he longed for someone who was at once a grandmother, a lovely mistress, and an accomplished secretary.

Three Other Novels

Nuptial Flight. The three other novels, *Children of the Market Place* (1922), *Nuptial Flight* (1923) published the same year as *Skeeters Kirby,* and *The Tide of Time* (1937) can be dealt with briefly. *Nuptial Flight* is the closest—in time, events, and characters taken from Masters's career—to the Skeeters Kirby trilogy. The title, suggesting a couple's romantic flight into marital bliss, is sarcastic.

Nuptial Flight begins with the immigration to Illinois of two Kentucky families. Soon the son of one and daughter of the other meet and are married. These two, Nancy and William Houghton, are Masters's grandparents, down to many details such as Nancy's illegitimate birth, the name Young in her family, her Irish blood, her working in an inn or tavern, and so on. They and their marriage are idealized in every way. But their story is only background to the story of their son and of his son—a story of misalliances and degenerating hopes and spirits.

Walter Scott Houghton, modeled on Hardin Masters, is the son of the two pioneers. Fanny Prentice, of New England Puritan stock, goes west to visit her sister and there meets Houghton. She schemes to capture him and does so; they have a tawdry wedding trip and a disastrous marriage. Their son Alfred, in life Edgar Lee, is a sensitive young man: "Alfred had been a dreamer all his life, and in his dreams music and the eternal feminine had played mastering parts" (163). The daughter Elaine is Masters's sister Madeline; the younger son Bertram is Masters's brother Thomas Davis Masters. Alfred becomes a violinist—Masters himself, he tells us in his autobiography, scraped at the violin as a boy and later as a young man in Chicago. Alfred meets Ida Ferris, a widow, twenty years his senior; she quickly snares him (both Ida and Fanny are described as spiders, devouring or poisoning their mates) and proceeds to exploit him and his musical talent.

One interesting variation in the autobiographical element of *Nuptial Flight* is in the relation between Alfred and Elaine. As in *Across Spoon River* and the novel *Skeeters Kirby,* the sister marries a wealthy young scion of a prominent family; he dies and leaves her financially secure; she travels in Europe and marries a European attracted by her money. In the other two books there are jealousies and resentments between brother and sister, but not in *Nuptial Flight.* As in *Mirage* Masters describes an affectionate and rewarding relationship with his mother, so in *Nuptial Flight* he presents an equally affectionate and rewarding relationship with his sister. The matter of which one, the son or the daughter, should go off to college is raised here as in the other books. It is settled easily by telescoping biography: Alfred goes to college at the very time that the elegant and wealthy young gentleman becomes interested in Elaine, so both siblings are happy. To a degree they become each other's support in adversity after both are married. Once Elaine expresses her con-

fidence in her brother: " 'You will go on, darling, to all triumphs.
I believe in you so. . . .' They held hands like lovers" (216). But
they are powerless to sustain each other. Elaine is exploited by her
second husband. Alfred's life is poisoned and consumed by his wife
Ida, the "spider." He meets and loves the beautiful Sybil, an accomplished pianist—again part Tennessee Mitchell and part "Pamela" or Lillian Wilson—but Ida destroys their love and Alfred's
artistic career, at least for the foreseeable future. The reader feels,
as Alfred does, that his great artistic success and acclaim are behind
him. The book ends in Spoon River, here called Whitehall. Fanny
and Ida, the two failed mother figures in Alfred's life, die, but
before her death Fanny and Alfred are reconciled. At the moment
of her death Alfred dreams of his wife's threatening presence; he
awakens to see the apparition of his mother and so is apprised of
her death. Finally, only Alfred's spiritual mother, the beloved grandmother Nancy Houghton, is left to comfort him.

Aside from its revelation of the author, *Nuptial Flight* is of small
interest as a novel. It does show Masters coming to terms with his
own biography and background, reconstructing his grandparents'
and his parents' courtships. It repeats the *Spoon River* motifs, which
presented the sordid small-town environment, the degeneration of
American life since the time of the pioneers, the corruption of
Christianity, and the failure of marriage as an institution. In many
respects it is an antimarriage tract. Its plot is a melange of one
idyllic marriage followed by two generations of melodramatic failures of marriage; and the separate marriage plots are poorly integrated, except that they occur in the same degenerating family of
Houghtons. Its style varies from hasty underwriting—"his mind
was gradually giving away" (13); to hasty overwriting—"As the
train speeds west [Fanny's] nature grows lighter, freer, as of wings
aërified from the mucilaginous secretions of the shell" (43–44).
Only the specialist will wish to consult it.

    The Tide of Time. *The Tide of Time* (1937), Masters's last
novel, is somewhat different from the earlier ones. Masters seems
to have taken more pains with it, and it appears to be less hastily
written; it is considerably longer than the other novels, though the
principal plot is devoted to the life of a single character, Leonard
Westerfield Atterbury; and the autobiography is somewhat more
disguised. Masters long contemplated a novel about his father, whose
modest career, despite his great gifts as a lawyer and his personal

magnetism, seems always to have puzzled his admiring son. In order to deal with the puzzle, Masters examines Hardin Masters's life as though it were his own. Again the grandparents, here Captain Squire Atterbury and his wife Dorcas (Squire is always a name, as in the actual Squire Davis Masters, though many readers and critics have assumed it to be a title), provide the sturdy pioneering base to the story. Their son, Leonard Westerfield Atterbury (he is always called by his double given name, Leonard Westerfield) is about half Hardin Masters and half Edgar Lee.

In this way Edgar Lee becomes (in fiction) the actual son of his grandmother, whose spiritual son he always felt himself to be. He also becomes the husband of his mother, although Leonard Westerfield's wife Adele Richland is not closely modeled upon Emma Masters. Adele is the hometown girl that young Atterbury left behind when he went away to college, much as Margaret George was left behind by Masters when he went to Knox College. In this respect it is perhaps Masters's trial of what his marriage to Margaret George would have been like: the answer given is that it would have been better than either his father's marriage to Emma or his own to Helen Jenkins, but not so very satisfactory after all.

In his teens Leonard Westerfield, like Masters, satisfies his sexual urges through the cooperation of maids employed by his mother (*ASR*, 89); but after the serving-maid Victoria Barnes is accidentally killed, his amorous adventures are remarkably restricted—for a Masters protagonist. At college he relives Masters's year at Knox College, including a brief pursuit by his middle-aged landlady—an event touched on in *Across Spoon River* and in *Skeeters Kirby* (113) and developed fully in *Nuptial Flight*. He has one later tumultuous affair, with the romantically named Sophronia, a beautiful, wealthy Chicago girl who, like Tennessee Mitchell, has been instructed in women's freedom by a liberated aunt. More interestingly, the nocturnal preludes to lovemaking are described in precisely the terms in which Masters describes his abortive flirtation with Isabel, the wealthy widow of his third cousin, in *Across Spoon River* (265). This same flirtation with "Isabel" is the subject of his early prose play, *The Trifler* (1908). In both the novel and the autobiography the hero's door is left significantly ajar, and the heroine passes hesitantly and noiselessly back and forth in the hallway. In life this episode occurred "shortly after my marriage," Masters reports in *Across Spoon River* (261); there was no consummation. But in *The Tide of Time*, after

nearly forty years, Leonard Westerfield takes Sophronia trium-
phantly to bed. He plans to marry Sophronia, but soon returns
instead to marry the hometown girl Adele.

Though he once begins to fear his "passional energy" (301), he
gives little evidence of passion from this point forward. Masters was
thinking here of his own "passional energy"—a characteristic to
which we will recur presently—not the more relaxed or resigned
character of Hardin Masters. It is just this lack of passion, partly
suppressed by his wife, who wanted him to take the safe and prof-
itable paths, that seems to be Masters's explanation for Hardin
Masters's failure to achieve great things. Leonard Westerfield, indeed, becomes mayor, judge, and congressman. But he feels helpless
to achieve any real good, unable to stem the tide which wastes the
lives of men and turns the friendly town of Ferrisburg from a Petersburg to a Lewistown: Spoon River.

Although Masters's private objective in *Tide of Time* was a fictional
biography of his father, his public objective, as he wrote to an
acquaintance, was an historical account of his section of Illinois
before the Civil War till about 1930, indicating the effects of the
Civil War on the town and on the nation.[4] His thesis is that the
Civil War in particular and other wars in general destroyed American
Jeffersonian democracy and substituted Hamiltonian centralization
and commercialism. There is much military history in the novel,
especially descriptions of Grant's campaigns, interesting in themselves but only remotely connected to the Leonard Westerfield plot.
There is also much social criticism of the inadequacies of twentieth-
century life in America. There are long editorials from the Ferrisburg
papers—a favorite topic of Masters, who wrote several editorials
himself in the *Lewistown News,* supporting his father's political aspirations. The rabble-rousing Editor Davis is Spoon River's Editor
Whedon with a change of name.

Masters like most authors thought his latest volume his best, at
least of its kind. This novel is a faithful picture of central Illinois,
faithful to his memories of the Spoon River country he portrayed
over and over in poetry and prose, fiction and nonfiction. It presents
much careful detail, but too much for easy assimilation. If the reader
perseveres to the end, however, he finds, this time, no epilogue but
a curious undercutting of the book's thesis and its social criticism.
For there Masters asserts that "America is a better country and life
in it is better than when Leonard Westerfield was born" (681). He

does not say why it is better, but he implies that it is so because of scientific advancements: that a woman is not likely "today" to die in childbirth; that a soldier is not so likely to die of typhoid fever like Samuel Atterbury, son of Leonard Westerfield and Adele; that techniques of birth control are coming into use. This mere assertion and implication are not enough to make Masters's often-professed meliorism convincing. It is an almost pathetic effort to find a bright spot in his picture of the gloom of twentieth-century American life.

The book ends, "But what always stands out, what makes a man's life somehow admirable, no matter how he has been caught and hindered, tortured, humiliated, and put aside? Perhaps nothing so much as that that man shall have done his duty. 'But what is your duty?' asked Goethe. 'The claims of the day,' he answered." This is the justification of Leonard Atterbury's career, of Hardin Masters's, and of Edgar Lee Masters's, as he was approaching his seventieth birthday, thirty-two years after the great success of *Spoon River.*

Children of the Market Place.   One novel, *Children of the Market Place* (1922), though the second to appear, has been reserved for last because it represents a different direction from the others in Masters's continuing search for his most congenial form. In the other novels Masters exploited his past and that of relatives or acquaintances (Mitch, Margaret George, his mother, his father, his sister Madeline Masters, Bill Reedy, Kit O'Brien). *Children of the Market Place,* though disguised as fiction, is the biography of Stephen A. Douglas (1813–1861), lawyer, politician, and orator, who opposed Lincoln in the still famous Lincoln-Douglas debates, which take place toward the end of the book. Clearly Douglas was a hero to Masters, one of many, literary and political. In Masters's political hagiography Jefferson and Washington come first, then Andrew Jackson, whom his grandfather had known, then Douglas.

The politics and political campaigns in *Children of the Market Place* are much better integrated than the military campaigns in *The Tide of Time,* because Douglas is presented as a close friend of the fictional protagonist, who is himself fascinated by the politics of the time and the area, central Illinois. The portrait of Douglas, supporter of Jefferson and protégé of Jackson, is interesting and fair, as is the description of the Lincoln-Douglas controversy. But the book wavers disconcertingly between biography and fiction, between the career of Douglas and that of James Miles, the narrator and fictional hero. Nevertheless, each has its interest, Miles's career as a variation on familiar autobiographical themes and Douglas's as the story of the "little giant," as he was known, an ambitious, energetic lawyer who won and lost a fortune in Chicago. Douglas's story is his own, not Masters's, though his support of Jeffersonian and Jacksonian principles, especially state sovereignty, was strongly endorsed by Masters.

Masters's autobiographical themes are least evident in this of all the novels. James Miles in the first place is an Englishman, whose father deserted his family and emigrated to America, where he left a fortune in Illinois land to his son. Still, Miles's mother was but eighteen when he was born, as Masters's mother was; as she died in childbirth, he was raised by his grandparents, another familiar note. Miles was born in 1815, which makes him about the age of Squire Davis Masters, with whom Edgar Lee so strongly associated himself. The voice of the hero-narrator Miles is that of Masters, and though the events are more melodramatic (for example, Miles's murder of a villain who has abused his beautiful half-sister of Negro blood), the attitudes and gestures are also Masters's. A typical attitude in *Across Spoon River* and in Masters's correspondence is revealed in his remark in *Across Spoon River* that all his achievements have been by brute force, "head lowered," his weight thrusting forward (152). Miles remarks: "I began to see myself as boring through opposition with lowered head and indomitable will" (112). Another characteristic of the Masters protagonist is the cold bath in the morning. In *Across Spoon River* Masters says this lifelong habit has kept him from illness (259). Young Miles, who spends his first Illinois winter in a rough cabin with his half-sister Zoe, relates that there "were mornings when the cold bath, which I could never forego, no matter what the circumstances were, tested my resolution."[5]

James Miles is again more like Hardin Masters in *The Tide of Time,* or more like Squire Davis Masters, than like Edgar Lee, their son and grandson, in his monogamous fidelity to his Tennessee wife Dorothy. She dies, however, and Miles meets and falls in love with the beautiful, cultured Mrs. Winchell who, like Becky Norris in *Skeeters Kirby* and *Mirage,* had married a much older man who was wealthy but sexually impotent. Miles, who has become independently wealthy through his inheritance and real estate speculation in Chicago, has leisure to devote to the arts. He studies etching;

Mrs. Winchell, whose name (again) is Isabel, studies painting. Soon Mr. Winchell—called Uncle Tom, in the author's attempt to relate his paternalism to Southern slavery, via Mrs. Stowe's novel—dies. Miles plans to marry Isabel, after a period of separation; but when he finally proposes he is insincere, and she feels it and gently rejects him. "The goddess had descended to me and here was I a witless fool" (380).

In the last chapter James Miles is eighty-four. His wealth has been lost in the Chicago fire. He lives in a boardinghouse, where, he says, "Miss Sharpe, delicate, spiritual, active of mind . . . comforts me" (455). Miss Sharpe is a second almost clairvoyant anticipation in 1921 of Miss Davis, Masters's secretary and friend in his Chelsea years (about 1931 through 1943) and of Ellen Masters, whom he married in 1926 and who nursed and sustained him through his final years. Or she is an emblem of an objective determinedly sought, the daughter/mother who would take care of him to the end. Miles, at the end of the novel, living in Chicago with a small but adequate income, meditates, "Yes, I believe I shall revise my will in favor of Miss Sharpe. Sometimes I suspect that she wants to marry me" (456). In the last lines of the novel, Miles rejects the wording of the epitaph on Douglas's tomb which exhorts his children "to obey the laws and support the Constitution." He accepts instead the words of another Masters hero: "Walt Whitman's admonition to the States: 'Obey little, resist much' " (468).

Chapter Nine

Biography: Setting the Record Straight

The Lure of Famous Men

Like *Spoon River Anthology* and most of the books that followed it, *Children of the Market Place* was an attempt to portray America through a faithful depiction of her representative men and women, towns and cities, realities and illusions. Stephen A. Douglas was the representative man, the Midwesterner by choice, the patriot politician who might have prevented the Civil War, which destroyed the old democratic federalism. The Midwest remained the representative region and Chicago the archetypal "Market Place." Behind this first major experiment in biography was sincere admiration for a political hero, into whose portrait went Masters's admiration and personal knowledge of another spokesman of the agrarian Midwest, William Jennings Bryan. Inevitably present also was the preeminent hero of Illinois politics, with roots in New Salem, adjacent to Petersburg, Douglas's great antagonist Abraham Lincoln.

Somewhat surprisingly, considering his later view in the biography *Lincoln: The Man* (1931), Masters's picture of Lincoln in *Children of the Market Place* was, though incomplete, appreciative: he was a worthy antagonist for Douglas in a long contest, an epic struggle between polarized forces, in which the Hamiltonian principle of the marketplace prevailed against the Jeffersonian rural values and permanently divided the nation. In *Spoon River* and *Mitch Miller* the Lincoln myth is also present, especially in the epitaph of Anne Rutledge in the former and the lecture delivered to the two boys by the Reverend Miller at the Lincoln monument in Springfield in the latter. The Lincoln myth, like the Tom Sawyer myth, grew up around Edgar Lee as a boy in his Petersburg years. Eventually he would have to deal with both of these myths in an effort to distinguish the myth from biography.

Biography did not just attract Masters as a literary genre; it was a central motivating force in his life. He points out in "The Genesis of Spoon River" that his consuming literary interest in high school was biography. He was fascinated by the stories of literary men, as he aspired to become an author himself. Passages already referred to can be recollected here: his finding excuses in high school to use the encyclopedia so that he could read the biographies of famous writers, and his fondness for the illustrated *Album of Authors*, which he "read to tatters," studying the authors' portraits and choosing Goethe and Shelley "as the best of all" (43).

So Masters early settled on two of his lifelong literary heroes by reading about their lives and examining their faces. At the same time his teacher Miss Fisher introduced him to Emerson: "Emerson, whose benign face and serene courage and penetrating eloquence gave us assurance that we were right," he later wrote in *The Living Thoughts of Ralph Waldo Emerson* (14). Emerson himself was an admirer of heroes, whom he praised in his *Representative Men* (1850), amply quoted in Masters's edition, which contains a thirty-five page introduction followed by 125 pages of selections. "In my own case [Emerson] led me to Swedenborg, Plato, Plotinus, and stood for me . . . against the theology that shrank from Goethe" (16).

In this same essay occurs Masters's mention of Washington as on a par with Jefferson. Although Jefferson is much more frequently praised in Masters's writing, here Masters names only Washington: "One wishes that [Emerson] had put Washington among his representative men, as the great rebel, the great republican, the great leader of a people seeking independence and liberty" (47). Here also occurs the name of another political hero, William Jennings Bryan, who had commanded Masters's absolute devotion and fervor in 1896. From that pinnacle in the presidential elections of 1896 and 1900, Bryan fell to the status of a lost leader, the object of Masters's scorn and hatred, as Bryan argued biblical fundamentalism against scientific Darwinism in the Scopes trial in 1925, the year of his death. By 1940, however, Masters had begun a reassessment: "Some day a fair and full picture will be given of William Jennings Bryan, who toured America in 1896 and 1900 trying to hold America to its noble path, its primal vision" (26). If Masters had kept his health for another few years, he would almost certainly have produced that biography of Bryan. In *More People* (1939), the year before *Emerson*, he had already published the poem "Fate of a Tribune," deploring the ignominious end of a nameless leader, evidently Bryan.

As it happened, the biographical strand in Masters, like the poetic strand and the fictional and the dramatic, reached its apogee in the gnomic portraits, slightly fictionalized, of *Spoon River Anthology*. Before *Spoon River*, Masters had written two early plays on historical personages, *Benedict Arnold* (1893) and *Maximilian* (1902). Between 1907 and 1914, he wrote probably ten plays (since they were not published, though he had many printed in the hope that they might interest actors, it is difficult to date certain plays), all based on the lives of real people, but more nearly fiction than biography. After *Spoon River*, there were only a couple of dramatic attempts—*Alum* (1919) and *The Manuscript of a Novel* (1922), based upon the manuscript of *Skeeters Kirby* lost in 1921 and then rewritten—until *Lee: A Dramatic Poem* in 1926. This poem, written mostly in rhymed pentameters, is neither very readable nor very actable, but it is a sincere homage to the great Virginia patriot whose namesake Masters claimed to be.

In 1927 appeared Masters's first full-length biography, *Levy Mayer and the New Industrial Era*, which he wrote more or less on commission from Mrs. Mayer, the widow of his subject. He wrote it also out of gratitude to Mrs. Mayer's brother, Masters's friend and associate Abraham Meyer, who had helped him greatly as his lawyer and friend at the time of his divorce from Helen Jenkins Masters.[1] It must have been very difficult for him to write, as Levy Mayer's career as a great corporation lawyer represented nearly everything that Masters opposed politically and economically. Here indeed Masters subjected himself to a rigorous discipline, repressing his own views, striving for objectivity. But it was not a congenial subject, and he had to repress too much of himself to allow for artistic achievement.

In 1928 came a third experiment in biography, *Jack Kelso, A Dramatic Poem*. Masters is more successful here, for he is dealing with traditional materials from his own Petersburg–New Salem background. Kelso was an actual New Salem character, a friend to Lincoln; but little was known about him. So Masters embellishes his career with fiction and with autobiography. In the fiction he exploits the Lincoln legend but uses it to Lincoln's disadvantage, implying that Lincoln as postmaster intercepted mail to Ann Rutledge (the spelling is "Ann" here, "Anne" in *Spoon River Anthology*) from his rival. Kelso calls Lincoln a "tyrant"; Kelso himself becomes a thieving railroad contractor, using inferior steel in a futile effort to become rich enough to marry the beautiful, wealthy Isabel (that name again). Of Lincoln, our most poetic president, Masters characteristically has Kelso say that words are "greater than" deeds, for Lincoln "won many" to his side through his words, though many hated what he did. Poetry "is like a pyramid," for it endures and it elevates the poet.[2] In the last few pages Lincoln is reviled for failing to give Ann Rutledge "a handsome stone" (259) for her grave.

In the related political poems of *Gettysburg, Manila, Ácoma* (1930), Masters once more approached the Lincoln problem in presenting John Wilkes Booth meditating the assassination. He was also continuing his long critique of American imperialism and oppression: of the South during and after the Civil War (in "Gettysburg"), of the Philippines (in "Manila"), of the American Indians (in "Ácoma").

Finally in 1931 Masters published his biography *Lincoln: The Man of the People*. He began the biography after reading Albert Beveridge's *Life of Abraham Lincoln* (1928), which was itself to a degree a response to Carl Sandburg's eulogy, *Abraham Lincoln: The Prairie Years* (1926). When the carefully assembled facts of Lincoln's life appeared in Beveridge's biography, Masters resolved to put down Lincoln and Sandburg at one blow. In a review of Beveridge's book dated 21 July 1928, Masters had proposed the need for "an analytical study of Lincoln . . . to reduce the enigmatic character of the man to its psychological elements. . . . It will require a mind of high and singular gifts to do this, but it . . . can be done by the right sort of genius."[3] How could he resist that self-challenge?

Masters dedicated *Lincoln: The Man* to Thomas Jefferson, listed Jefferson's attributes, and offered the opinion that he was America's greatest president. From the outset, then, Masters's partisan viewpoint is unmistakable. Throughout, the views of the Jeffersonian-Democrat Masters are argued and extolled at the expense of Republican Lincoln. His point is not to be pettily vindictive but to set the record straight, to disabuse his countrymen, as Masters himself had become disabused, of the comforts of the Lincoln myth, and to show them the superior virtues of the Jeffersonian way. It was very like his purpose in *Spoon River*: to look behind the surfaces of village (that is, American) life, to expose its wounds and festering sores that they might be healed.

One of the most interesting of his observations about Lincoln is one to which he often alluded, as in the poetry-as-pyramid image from *Jack Kelso*. It is that Lincoln's fame rests on his power as a poet; Lincoln was a hypocrite who enraptured men's souls with his Jeffersonian words while stealing their liberties through his Hamiltonian actions. Masters, as a lover of poetry, had been one of the deceived. As he wrote in *Across Spoon River*, the Gettysburg Address as poetry was a "miracle worker" (172).

Literary Lives and Legends

These views of Lincoln as poet are of a piece with Masters's attitude toward Whitman: what he most admired in Whitman from the first was not his poetry *qua* poetry, but his large, Jeffersonian view of America and the American potential (*ASR,* 336). For Christmas 1942, just a year before the illness that ended his active career, Masters sent to a friend, Mrs. Gertrude Claytor, a copy of his biography *Whitman* (1937), with the enigmatic comment that Whitman was "our best poet in his way, but not so good as Poe and Emerson—in any way."

Masters's comments suggest that he conceived of poetry as a powerful political weapon, a medium for affecting men's minds through the power of language, but at the same time as a medium to be regarded with suspicion when so used. Lincoln and Whitman both spoke political wisdom, but Lincoln's words failed to conform to the political realities of his presidency; and the political realities of Masters's time failed to answer to the optimistic predictions of Whitman's words. Poe's lyric, apolitical voice offered no such problems. Emerson's judicious, philosophic voice controlled his Jeffersonian politics. Shelley's political, lyric voice captivated Masters for many years. Goethe's rational criticism of human foibles gave his voice the greatest authority for Masters, though Masters also wrote of another rational, critical, humorous voice, Chaucer's, "this Chaucer, with whom I feel as much kinship as any poet" (inscribed in a gift copy of Chaucer). Indeed, as John Cowper Powys insisted in the 1915 lecture which so terrified Masters,[4] there are resemblances to Chaucer in *Spoon River*. But Masters, convinced that he could do better than *Spoon River* in some other direction, was not content to maintain the relative detachment of the Spoon River portraits. His own political nature, his reformist urges, his legal training, did not permit him to ignore the temptations of political and social commentary. As he wrote in a letter about 1922 concerning his novel *Children of the Market Place*, he had "the real intercessor's passion for nailing lies and rescuing obscured Titans."[5] He might have added, "the real intercessor's passion" for discovering truth and debunking false heroes. *Children of the Market Place*, in which he attributed to Douglas all the heroic qualities he had earlier assigned to Bryan in the campaign of 1896, was a rescue mission. *Lincoln: The Man* was an exposé. It was so extreme and denunciatory that it probably did more to discredit the popular image of Masters than that of Lincoln.

Unlike Chaucer, who wrote with a realistic detachment that harbored no illusions as to the world he inhabited, Masters, like most of us, cherished his illusions and was therefore subject to bitter disillusionment: with family, with lovers, with law partners, with friends; with Bryan, with Mark Twain, with Lincoln. Reversals in attitude of 180 degrees are common in Masters's career, sometimes more than once with the same person, as with his mother whom he loved and hated and loved in succession; or Theodore Roosevelt, whom he reviled and then admired and then detested; or Bryan, whom he worshiped and then despised and finally admired. Characteristically he became personally, emotionally involved with everything that interested him—or to put it another way, what interested him was what he could relate immediately and personally to himself.

A contemporary poet, Vachel Lindsay.   The biography *Vachel Lindsay, A Poet in America* (1935) was another rescue mission. As a contemporary Midwestern poet, already neglected since his suicide in 1931, the year of Masters's *Lincoln*, Lindsay was a remarkably appropriate subject. Masters could identify with Lindsay as a neglected Midwestern poet; he could excoriate his shabby treatment by publishers, particularly the Eastern publishing establishment; he could, and did, voice his own prejudices while praising and defending Lindsay. Yet the subjective element, expressed as sympathy for another writer like himself and no longer a competitor, makes this Masters's best biography.

His firmest insistence in explaining Lindsay's failure as a poet is that "Art and poetry must have logic. Lack of logic was the vice which defeated his art ambitions, and weakened his verse."[6] He laments Lindsay's choice of "Hebraism instead of Hellenism" (178), by which he meant evangelical Christianity or Puritanism, instead of the neoclassicism of Jefferson and the other founders of the republic (251, 266). He refers to Lindsay's saying to him once that Masters's "literary paternity was the science of law, and his that of art." Masters seems ready enough to have his own work characterized by "the logic of legal thinking," for was not "Goethe . . . a lawyer?" (264). He finds in Lindsay's career many of the same problems that beset his own: how his mother "had marked his life so deeply"; the need to revolt "against the American village"; the frustrations of youthful idealism and energy in "a civilization of small merchants and the parasitism of lawyers, and the hypocrisy of politicians" (190).

He wishes Lindsay might have had some sustaining force, some focusing agent in his life: "Truly it was necessary for him to choose one man" (Emerson, Shelley, Goethe, Bryan?), or "rather one great object of devotion [Jeffersonianism?] around which he could accrete his various passions and idolatries" (177); "When I was a youth there in Illinois, except for the sustaining voices of Whitman and Emerson we should have sunk to the dregs" (199). Perhaps Whitman especially might have saved Lindsay, for "the two men shared many beliefs" (256); "Whitman and Lindsay were both natural celibates; both were old men at fifty. Both were victims of the Civil War, and both idolators of Lincoln" (258). Most valuable, probably, "would have been a lover, that is some man or woman who could have drawn him out and along the way, and by the exercise of affectionate intuition shown him how much there was and how much there was not to his visions" (196)—someone to do for him what Tennessee Mitchell did for Masters. Yet even without these advantages, Masters recognizes that Lindsay, "when the sincerity of his feeling, his passion, burned all the non-essentials away, and left nothing but the pure jewel of his imagination as the residue, even amid the ashes . . . succeeded with verse" (192). When Masters sent a gift copy of *Vachel Lindsay* to Mrs. Claytor, he inscribed it as "this record of a great poet." He and Lindsay, Masters felt, had much in common.

No careful Masters-watcher could have been surprised when he published his autobiography the next year, 1936. Yet he was at a peak of biographical production. *Poems of People* came also in 1936, some of the poems celebrating heroes such as Washington and Jefferson, others ordinary people treated as fictions. The novel about his father, *The Tide of Time*, and a study, *Whitman*, were published in 1937, along with Masters's epic poem of America, *The New World*. In 1938 Masters published *Mark Twain*, in 1939 *More People*, and in 1940 *Emerson*.

Writers and teachers: Whitman, Twain, Emerson.   The final biographies—of Whitman, Twain, and Emerson—are all of literary heroes of his youth; his admiration for Twain dates from Petersburg and for Whitman and Emerson from his high school days in Lewistown. The studies of both Whitman and Emerson are essentially introductions to the poets, composed largely of their own writing. But both writers Masters presents more nearly as great Americans than as great poets. Whitman is the patriot and political philosopher—"a great liberal . . . a prophet of democracy," but no great poet.[7] Emerson, the political and moral philosopher "was not skilled in rhyme, his sense of metre . . . faulty. But those who look for . . . philosophy and meaning in poetry will not mind these faults. . . ."[8]

Mark Twain, A Portrait (1938) may well have begun, like the others, as an act of homage. In *Poems of People* (1936) the poem "The House Where Mark Twain Was Born" contains no trace of animosity; it is nostalgic, even sentimental, yearning for the old "village cottages" in which "a wonder boy" (any yet unrecognized genius such as Twain, or Lincoln, or Masters) could "dream by the kitchen stove." But as Masters reassessed Twain from the point of view of Jeffersonian-agrarian politics, which had become over the years more and more a central, conscious, critical criterion, Twain appeared lacking. In Masters's view his great lack was his failure to become the satirist of his time. We have already discussed above Masters's consciousness of resemblances between himself and Twain. His disappointment and bitterness in Twain become more poignant as we reflect on what Masters might have accomplished had he been endowed with Twain's gifts for humor and satiric prose. He could not forgive Twain for failure to exploit those gifts for the betterment of America in his own time. Similarly he could not forgive him as an artist for allowing his wife Olivia to censor his manuscripts and surround him "with influences that emasculated him."[9] He was fresh from confessing in *Across Spoon River* his own succumbing to uxorial censorship. His first wife thought a poem he had written seemed to describe licentiousness, so Masters rewrote it to accord with Mrs. Masters's "scruples" (253). Yet Masters finally rebelled and left his wife, as Twain did not. And Masters fully exploited his own gifts in his efforts to improve the nation.

Biography of a Region: *The Sangamon*

Masters's last prose book, *The Sangamon* (1942) resembles a large body of his work in being a reminiscence of the Sangamon River area where he lived as a boy in and around Petersburg. Ostensibly a history of the region, one of the Rivers of America series written by eminent writers of the period, the book was a final nostalgic reminiscence from Masters's seventy-fourth year, and so it is more nearly autobiography than history. Most interesting historically is the description of New Salem, about two miles from Petersburg, where Masters had played as a boy and which is intimately bound up with the myth of Lincoln. Nearly 20 percent of the pages of *The Sangamon* contain some mention of Lincoln; but here there is none of the vituperation of *Lincoln: The Man*, which would have ruined the affectionate, nostalgic tone of the book. Rather, Masters maintains an objective attitude, presenting Lincoln through the eyes of the people of New Salem, on the whole favorably.

Most interesting biographically is Masters's narrative of his winter visit to Oakford with Dreiser just before the Spoon River poems began to appear: "We then went to the Oakford Cemetery. I wanted to note the names of people I had known in the many long summers that I had worked on the Masters farm for my grandfather" (107). Also of interest is Masters's account of his near drowning in the millrace of New Salem (72–73), not told elsewhere. Masters devotes several pages to "Vachel Lindsay . . . the most important figure native to Illinois" (124). Lincoln was born in Tennessee, Douglas in New England, Masters in Kansas. That left only Carl Sandburg among the more obvious heroes of Illinois to compete for the honor. But Sandburg is nowhere mentioned in the text, though he lurks in the background as the biographer of Lincoln and competitor of Lindsay and of Masters. Sandburg's birthplace, Galesburg, is mentioned three times, with the emphasis on its difference from New Salem, Petersburg, Sandridge: "Knox County, where the Swedes became predominant at Galesburg . . . a different country, as alien to New Salem and Sandridge as are the Ozarks" (33). There is also an audible echo, intentional or not, of Sandburg's poem "The Grass" in this sentence which concludes a paragraph on Lincoln: "Men can be piled in death as thick as cordwood at Gettysburg, Verdun or in Flanders, the game of life is always taken care of by nature . . ." (213). It seems almost a translation of Sandburg's "Pile the bodies high . . . at Gettysburg / And pile them high at Ypres and Verdun. / . . . I am the grass. / Let me work."

Interlarded with the prose of *The Sangamon* are poems taken from other late volumes by Masters: *Poems of People, More People* (1939), *Illinois Poems* (1941), *Along the Illinois* (1942). Masters changed or adapted the poems for the new context, usually without improvement. They illustrate Masters's late poetic style, which is close to that of *Songs and Sonnets* (1910) before *Spoon River* and close to that of *Songs and Satires* (1916) after *Spoon River*. The poem adapted from "Flowers of Illinois" in *Illinois Poems* (1941) illustrates some of the characteristics. The setting is rural, the tone nostalgic, the subject reminiscences of farm and village life of central Illinois in the 1870s and 1880s. The style is narrative, descriptive, expository, and even lyrical. It is rhymed, alliterative, but hastily written or revised, with resultant grammatical and syntactical problems.

Punctuation and metrics aside, the later poems, like the later prose, are celebrations of a lost Eden: the New Salem of Lincoln's time, the Petersburg of Masters's childhood, his grandparents' farm— Masters's haven till he was forty—the unspoiled prairie of the Indians and the pioneers, America of the Jeffersonian dream. The details of grammar and prosody were unimportant (as he said of Emerson, "those who look for . . . philosophy and meaning in poetry will not mind these faults"); the thing that mattered was the message: we must preserve what is left of the old values. If there is a single theme in Masters's writing, this is it. It is implicit even in *Spoon River Anthology*. Lewistown implied the loss of Petersburg; Spoon River implied the idyllic Sangamon.

As a child in Petersburg, Masters compared his quarrelsome parents, his orderless home unfavorably with the harmony and order at his grandparents' farm. When he went to Lewistown, he had just lost his best "chum" Mitch Miller and so looked back nostalgically to Petersburg. His parents looked back to the peace before the Civil War and his grandparents to the politics of Jackson and Jefferson. Masters's retrospective bent was established early. Radical as he seemed and thought himself to be in his social and political criticism, his instincts and his psychology were essentially conservative, even reactionary as he struggled all his life to reaffirm the principles and values of Jefferson and of his own pioneering grandparents.

When the literary world was saluting *Spoon River Anthology* as a step forward into the twentieth century, away from slavish imitation of nineteenth-century models, they hailed its author as leader of the vanguard. When Masters confided to his friends that he thought he could do better in some other direction, he may well have known that the only other direction was retrospective, fighting a rear-guard action against the forces of the marketplace, imperialism, war, repression, with the hope of preserving and augmenting individual freedom.

Chapter Ten
Across Spoon River
The Autobiography

After experiments in autobiography as poetry, drama, novel, biography, and even history, Masters finally published his bona fide autobiography in 1936, the year after *Vachel Lindsay*. In 1933 he had written for Mencken's *American Mercury* the long article "The Genesis of Spoon River" and had published a nonfiction history, *The Tale of Chicago* (1933). These two provided the basis for the autobiography. As the title, *Across Spoon River*, implies, it is a partial autobiography, covering the years up to *Spoon River Anthology* and attempting to explain how he came to write it. It is a look back across Spoon River, which was still his Rubicon. At first this Rubicon was almost the literal stream, the Spoon, which runs by Lewistown, and its "crossing" was Masters's flight from Lewistown to Chicago in the winter of 1891–92; gradually it became *Spoon River*, the *Anthology*, whose singular success committed him to poetry instead of the law and determined his whole subsequent career.

Memory versus Imagination. As a backward look from the age of sixty-seven, given Masters's rational lawyer's training and disposition, *Across Spoon River* became a rationalization of his career, which he saw as a struggle between will and fate, with himself making his way through sheer determination: "only my will," he says, brought him to his goals (60). His characteristic pose was curiously bovine—"head . . . down . . . thrusting . . . forward" (120); his every achievement was by great effort, "head lowered" (152); each forward motion was made in opposition (273), "head . . . bowed" aggressively (278); he was himself the major "influence" affecting his career (287). The emphasis on fate we have already pointed to: "strands of fate" (20, 34), and the phrases "fateful" series of events (63), turns of "the wheel of fortune," the "fated" search for "the eternal feminine" (170), and so on; and there is a parallel emphasis on Masters's ill luck: "great luck" never came to him (120), or "fell [his] way"(156); in his persistent struggle he was granted "no luck" (278).

Masters's self-portrait is not very flattering. But the details are at times disarmingly frank: he acknowledges with regret his own "self-pity" (165), and he admits to self-hate commingled with it (209). Masters appears to be attempting an honest account of his first forty-five years—of the origins of *Spoon River Anthology*. He simply cannot help selecting certain emphases which will show his client (himself) to his judge and jury (his readers) as rising in the democratic tradition from humble beginnings and, despite adversity, to fame and fortune (and sexual conquests), through strength of character, manliness, and brains.

However, many later readers would not agree that he had no luck. For example, he was fortunate in his adoring grandmother. He was fortunate in the simultaneous influence of a remarkable teacher, Mary Fisher, and his learned and talented girl friend, Margaret George. He was also blessed with notably helpful male friends, first Ernest McGaffey and later William Marion Reedy, as well as Sandburg and Dreiser. In fact within the final ten pages, Masters acknowledges his "high fortune" that he has had such friends "as . . . Reedy" (409). All the other names he mentions here— including Powys, H. L. Mencken, Harriet Monroe, Eunice Tietjens—were of primary value to him after *Spoon River*.

Finally, after summarizing the ugliness and perils of his youth, Masters writes that he survived with the help of his friend Margaret George; that he had good luck "after all" through the intercession of his "brother the god" (411–12). Here, in the epilogue to *Across Spoon River,* there are several mentions of this daemon. The first is in association with his grandmother—in his consciousness "of a good daemon, a brother god," deriving he suggests from the affection of his grandmother (399). The second is in association with Margaret George (paraphrased just above). The third is in association with Reedy and the fourth with an unnamed woman companion. No one could expect to have two such friends as Reedy in one "lifetime"; but writing in 1935 Masters was convinced that his brother-the-god had "returned" (414). Reedy died in 1920. The explanation of the return is vague and mystical: "my brother . . . metamorphosed [into] a goddess . . ." understanding and devoted, loving and forgiving (416–17). This metamorphosed goddess, bringer of good fortune and poetic inspiration, must be Alice Elizabeth Davis, who came to Masters's apartment at the Hotel Chelsea to help him with his Whitman biography (1937), took a room nearby, and stayed as his devoted companion and friend until his illness in 1943. The intervening years he once said were the most contented and peaceful of his life.

Related to his apprehension of "my brother the god" is Masters's insistence, also in the epilogue, that the greatest force in his life has been his "imagination" (398). In trying to describe his imaginative life, he says that behind material objects he has always been aware of things "immaterial"; he speaks of his "mystical eyes" from which he viewed his surroundings and adds that mysterious incandescences and far off places beckoned him in his youth (400). As he describes it, the imagination in which he has lived is not a synthesizing, creative faculty that perceives relationships and order, but a mystical, yearning quality beckoning him onward toward the satisfaction of desires. It is strangely close to his own "towering will" by which Masters claims to have been ruled (405), continuously setting him new personal goals and directing him almost single-mindedly to their achievement. In his final comment on the imagination, Masters very nearly abjures it. He describes different kinds of poetry. One is the poetry "of . . . imagination," poetry that calms or stimulates the emotions. The highest poetry, however, the poetry he has devoted himself to, is poetry based on "the truth which is the beautiful," and which demonstrates spiritual laws and their retributive force (413–15). The province of poetry was truth; if it dealt with the spirit, it did so not as a seeking for a profounder reality than that of the phenomenal world, but as an effort to "prove" the spirit's knowable and known "laws"; and these laws were analogues of Aristotelian and Jeffersonian—classic and neoclassic—jurisprudence.

In the epilogue Masters refers repeatedly to Goethe, as the transcendent imagination interpreting human love. And although Masters thought of himself as a man of imagination, he really was not. He was too essentially sane. To deny that Masters was a man of imagination, however, is only to say that his true gifts, his genius, lay elsewhere. Besides his remarkable memory, he had a remarkable talent for acquiring significant things to remember. He had not only, as Tietjens pointed out, "read everything and . . . remembered everything," but he had also experienced a tremendous amount.

This drive to experience he analyzes in *Across Spoon River* jut after his comments on imagination. He calls attention to an element in his nature that was constantly pursuing a foreseen objective. He was born, he says, "with exhaustless, continuous energy," which he inherited from his grandmother (402). Though he preferred to think of it as his living in the imagination, or as his domination by "a towering will," or his being guided by a "brother god," Masters himself seemed to feel that this "precious and abounding vitality" (86) was the secret of his genius. It drove him to wide experience, it filled his memory with usable material, it gave him a sense of direction and destiny and the self-confidence to persevere toward the goals he sought. It even gave him the charisma and charm of the confident, determined man, which all his life won him friends and admirers.

Yet such energy was not an unmixed blessing. The energetic soul will be conscious of his will, but also of its frustration by an unkind fate and by individuals who may have "wills" or directions of their own. He will be conscious, like Masters, of "a voice" saying to him " 'hurry, hurry' " (192), of a daemon, another self, impelling him forward. He will wish for release from the inner goad, the frantic pace, and he will find release only for fleeting moments in sensation and the achievement of particular goals and, if he is lucky and an artist, in the contemplation of "the universal in the particular"[1]— which for Goethe defined the creative act.

In *Spoon River Anthology,* Masters was able to grasp the particulars of his remembered Lewistown (augmented by his memories of Petersburg) and its townspeople with sufficient authority to encompass the universal. Reedy evidently recognized at once what was occurring and encouraged him. Eventually Masters himself recognized the universal quality in what had commenced as forcefully etched individual character sketches. No longer satisfied with his angry and loving portraits, which were merely accurate and true, he began to seek in his characters those particulars which would reveal the universal. The major defects of *Spoon River Anthology* and of Masters's subsequent work may be traced to his effort to illustrate the universal by means of the particular—in his own words, to "draw the macrocosm by portraying the microcosm" (*ASR,* 339)—rather than to examine the particular that it might reveal the universal. The distinction is crucial. The emphasis of the seeker is on the particular, the means, "the way" (Tao); the emphasis of the knower is on the universal, the end, the destination. Both emphases are common in Masters. In *Spoon River* the former predominates because the characters themselves are seekers and because the form emphasizes that even when they believe they have discovered and try to inculcate universal truths, these are their truths and not necessarily the poet's. Only when the speaker's voice becomes the poet's, when the poet attempts to inculcate discovered truths, does the form fail and the art diminish into didacticism. Had Masters trusted his memories and his emotions as he did in parts of *Spoon River Anthology,* he might have sustained the promise which Reedy, Ezra Pound, Mencken, and others felt in the early Spoon River portraits.

"Give me a Voice." In *A Poet's Life,* Harriet Monroe quotes Masters's complaint about the reception of *The Great Valley,* his first book of poems written after *Spoon River:* "I wish a big critic would come along, and if I can't write I wish he'd say so. I'd quit so quick everybody could hear the silence." About the same time, before he left his family in the summer of 1917, he wrote to Monroe, "Give me a Voice, and I will follow it. I have one in my daemon, but for a long time he has left me alone. I am looking for him any time."[2] Ten years later, six years after Reedy's death in 1920, he wrote in a letter to the *New York Evening Post Literary Review* that America had had no "real critic" of poetry since Reedy, but that if such a critic should appear he would respect his judgment.[3]

The difficulty is that a "real critic" to a given artist is likely to be defined as one who can, where others cannot, discern the true merit of that artist's best work. Masters had at least the three able and respected critics, Reedy, Pound, and Mencken—Monroe is a fourth, Tietjens a fifth—who could and did discern the true merit of *Spoon River* and were equipped to offer valuable advice (for example, Monroe's plea to Masters to open *Songs and Sonnets* not with the conventional "Launcelot and Elaine" narrative but with the more "modern" poem "Silence"). But Reedy was Masters's friend. Masters did not actually meet Mencken till the 1920s (despite the letter of introduction from Dreiser in 1914). The editors of *Poetry* were Midwesterners, with a bias in favor of Illinois poets; yet both Monroe and Tietjens tried, in vain, after 1915, to explain to Masters the superiority of his *Spoon River* poems. Ezra Pound, however, did write him directly, advising and warning. Pound had just given advice and assistance to the great Irish poet William Butler Yeats; he was soon to edit *The Waste Land* (1922) for T. S. Eliot. Here was a "big critic" whose doctrine of imagism had already influenced Amy Low-ell in New England, George Sterling on the West Coast, and Sand-burg and probably Masters himself in the Midwest—a "Voice," that came to Masters's ear in 1915, full of sound poetic advice. Somehow Masters was unable to recognize it.

One reason seems to be that he was unsure of his own voice. Or rather he recognized his true voice but could not comprehend that his true voice was also his proper poetic voice. Firmly believing that literature, particularly poetry, demanded a high formal style, Masters developed and used such a style until he sent to Reedy what he considered obvious nonpoems in his own voice. Reedy's enthu-siasm persuaded him to continue the *Anthology*. But, especially in the later epitaphs, the reader senses a constant struggle between Masters's own voice—homely, bantering, angry, questioning—and his "literary" voice—elevated, serious, philosophical, exclamatory. By the time he reached the epilogue his literary voice had conquered. This is the source of his long search for the other direction from *Spoon River,* the true arc of his circle, which would allow full expres-sion to his literary voice. He found it in both prose and poetry, particularly in the blank verse dramatic monologues and narratives of *Domesday Book* and many later works. But this was not the voice people were listening for, a familiar voice speaking their own lan-guage, which they had heard in the early poems of the *Spoon River Anthology.*

They were to hear echoes of it in *The New Spoon River* (1924) and, more faintly (with a Chinese-American accent), in *Lichee Nuts* (1930). But they never heard it again in its first full vigor. Not that Masters's true voice was silenced. He continued to speak and write in his own voice all his life. This was the voice for which he was famed among friends and acquaintances as a raconteur, a storyteller with a gift for character and significant detail. It was the voice of his voluminous correspondence, which must equal or surpass in word-count his impressive production, published and unpublished, in his literary voice.

Masters's letters to his many friends are full of typos and solecisms, but they also have a free, fresh, impromptu flavor rather like the best of the *Spoon River* poems. Many of the letters, in fact, are signed with the names of Masters's favorite Spoon River characters, Lucius Atherton—more often Lewd—or Lute Puckett (possibly the ima-ginary illegitimate son of Lydia Puckett of Spoon River, one of

Lucius Atherton's conquests). Other aliases are Hod Putt (title of the first *Spoon River* epitaph), Elmer Chubb (a Christian bigot prominent in *Lichee Nuts*), Harley Prowler, and Sir Bors. The familiar ring of some of these names reminds us that the original *Spoon River* poems were just such impromptu first-person statements of opinion or outrage spoken by an alter ego or persona that allowed the poet to objectify his feelings. Thus Masters's "true voice" in his poetry is, oddly, the voice of a persona. In his letters to intimate friends he could speak without the persona, though he often chose to use one mask or another to allow him to speak more directly or satirically or outlandishly than he might otherwise. In the letters he could easily or casually assume or remove this transparent mask. But in the best of the *Spoon River* poems the mask was not transparent. The force and conviction of an epitaph derived from the authenticity of the persona. Whenever the face of the poet began to show through the mask, the voice lost its liberating simplicity and artlessness and became stuffy and didactic.[4] And when Reedy revealed his authorship, Masters stood exposed with all his masks removed and with small possibility of ever again achieving that kind of distance which allowed his unpoetic voice to speak for once authentic poetry.

Yet the fact that he continued to use that voice in his letters to his intimate friends, as well as the now transparent pseudonyms of Lewd Atherton and others shows that he recognized theirs as his true voice and their subject matter—the remediable evils of the world and the human need for love and sexual fulfillment—as his major themes.

Masters Across *Spoon River*

Once *Spoon River* was published in book form, Masters recognized that his career as a lawyer had ended. He had been living with his wife and three children during those "affluent days" preceding *Spoon River*. They "had several servants, a cook and a second maid . . . a janitor, . . . a yardman [and] . . . a chauffeur."[5] How was he to support his family in their accustomed comfort? He must continue as a writer and exploit his fame as a means of survival.

Spoon River had already insured that survival, though not in the bread-and-butter sense of providing an adequate income. But it did insure him a major voice in the American poetic renaissance and a permanent place in American literary history. Willard Thorp, coeditor of the definitive *Literary History of the United States,* chose an astrological metaphor to sum up the effect of *Spoon River Anthology:* "Several planets conjoined to make the book . . . one of the most momentous in American literature."[6] It was not, like Thomas Paine's *Common Sense* or Harriet Beecher Stowe's *Uncle Tom's Cabin,* momentous for its political or social effects. Though it undoubtedly had such effects, they are not easily identifiable or traceable. Its chief significances were literary. First was its effect on the reading audience of its time. Second was its immediate effect on other writers of its time. Third was its long-range effect on the form and content of American poetry.

The quantitative effect of *Spoon River Anthology* on the readers of its time is obvious. It was simply the most widely read and discussed book of poetry that had yet appeared in America. It was therefore read by many—from whatever motives from curiosity to titillation—who had perhaps never before read an entire poem, much less a book of poetry. Its popular and critical acclaim each reinforced the other, and each depended in part upon the book's frankness in the treatment of sex and other "sordid" qualities of average American lives. *Spoon River,* therefore, in these quantitative terms alone, enormously expanded both the audience and the subject matter of American poetry. What Masters had done was to re-create the small town and the American small-town experience just at the moment when the transition from the village to the metropolis was a central fact of American life. A huge majority of the literate population had moved, like Masters, to the impersonal city. They were uprooted and consciously or unconsciously looked back nostalgically to the community of the small town. This was the remembered condition in which every face was familiar and bore a known name. One knew one's place in relation to the community. What one did had an observable effect on others. How different· was the new urban experience in which a familiar face was a distinct surprise, where one was no more than a cipher in the mass, a cipher whose actions were unimportant to others and scarcely even noticed! If one regretted the loss of village community, one could take comfort in relief from immediate daily exposure to dullness, pettiness, futility in the lives of acquaintances, friends, and even one's own family.

These were among the psychological necessities and effects which produced the literary phenomenon too neatly summed up in the catchwords, "revolt from the village." What appeared in American literature as a renunciation and disparagement of village life was more nearly its reverse. The new urbanites—Masters, Sherwood Anderson, Sinclair Lewis, and their audiences—were trying to recapture their roots and to rationalize their new environment in relation to the old.

Spoon River was recognized immediately as the archetypical Midwestern small town by the reading populace, including admiring and envious writers. Walter Havighurst in *The Heartland: Ohio, Indiana, Illinois* relates that "in the spring of 1915, a friend had given [Sherwood] Anderson a copy of the Masters poems [*Spoon River Anthology*], which he read all night. A few months later he began working freshly on the Winesburg book," *Winesburg, Ohio* (1919).[7] What Anderson must have felt as he read all night was a clue to the possibility of coming to terms with his own Midwest village background, of discovering in his own backyard, so to speak, known people to be developed into living characters, of finding in ordinary village lives truths of American life and of the human heart.

The direct effects of *Spoon River* on other writers than Anderson are certain, though not always convincingly demonstrable. A few examples and hints of their connections can be give here. Ezra Pound is well known today for having been a friend, critic, and teacher of poets, among them W. B. Yeats, T. S. Eliot, and William Carlos Williams. When he recognized in the early *Spoon River* poems for the first time in the twentieth century a distinctly American poetic voice, and when he consolidated his views on how Masters's promise might be maintained and certain pitfalls avoided, he was developing his own critical principles, which he later imposed most successfully and famously upon Eliot's *The Waste Land.*

John Dos Passos as a student editor of the *Harvard Monthly* wrote a review of Pound's *Catholic Anthology* (1915), in which he found Masters's poem "Hortense Robbins" from *Spoon River* the best thing in the Pound anthology.[8] He had not, while at Harvard, determined he would be a writer (he was planning a career in architecture). Yet when he published his own masterpiece *U.S.A.* in the 1930s, it had certain subtle resemblances to *Spoon River Anthology.* Where Masters treated the microcosm, Dos Passos treated the macrocosm. Both used a variety of portraits, fictional and nonfictional, to portray American life. Both used cinematic techniques—Masters close-ups and dissolves, Dos Passos "Camera Eye" and "Newsreels"—and a recognizable thread of autobiography. One of *U.S.A.*'s central fictional characters, Eleanor Stoddard, bears a striking resemblance to *Spoon River*'s Hortense Robbins (and may owe something as well to Masters's Elenor Murray of *Domesday Book*).

Thornton Wilder's most successful work, the play *Our Town* (1938), manifestly derives from *Spoon River*. Spoon River, Illinois, has become Grover's Corners, New Hampshire; the villagers have died but return to reenact typical scenes of village life; the living are portrayed as well-intentioned but blind to meaning in their lives. At the beginning of act 2, Wilder acknowledges his debt with a reference to "one of those Middle West poets" and a paraphrase of "Lucinda Matlock." The play also seems to have been influenced by Anderson's Winesburg version of Spoon River. In turn *Our Town* influenced the bare-stage setting of performances of *Spoon River* in the 1960s and 1970s.

Chiefly through Sherwood Anderson during their association in the mid-1920s, William Faulkner derived literary nourishment from *Spoon River*. Faulkner is perhaps the American writer closest to Masters in developing and exploiting a geographical microcosm (Yoknapatawpha County) which could preserve in literature the village life and the sectional mores, as the villages gave way to the city, and the sections to the amalgamated United States.

In the 1920s Robinson Jeffers, twenty years his junior, became an admirer and friend of Masters. In 1926 the two poets met at Jeffers's home in Carmel, California, where, with the poet George Sterling, they planted a symbolic tree, signifying the poet's indissoluble connection with the land. From the microcosmic village, the free verse experiments and the social satire of *Spoon River,* Jeffers went on to the macrocosmic earth, the long free-verse lines, the cosmic irony of his best work.

Among the works of other writers affected by *Spoon River* are Sinclair Lewis's *Main Street* (1920); Zona Gale's *Miss Lulu Bett* (1920); E. W. Howe's *The Anthology of Another Town* (1920), whose very title acknowledges the debt; William March's *Company K* (1933); John Steinbeck's *The Pastures of Heaven* (1932). The Wisconsin poet August Derleth was a great admirer of Masters; unquestionably the Sac Prairie people of his *Selected Poems* (1945) owe much to the Spoon River example. As we approach the present we find the connections more tenuous, but Dylan Thomas's radio play of a Welsh village, *Under Milkwood* (1954), and Robert Lowell's character sketches in *Life Studies* (1959) have observable relationships to *Spoon River,* as do the short free-verse sketches from the Midwest of Dave Etter's *Go Read the River* (1966). This last poet also appears in *Heartland, Poets of the Midwest* (1967), an anthology of the work of twenty-nine Midwest poets—among them Robert Bly, Gwendolyn Brooks, William Stafford, James Tate, and James Wright—all influenced in indefinable ways by *Spoon River Anthology* over half a century earlier, with its sense of place, its crudity, its American speech, its social protest, its interior monologues, and its open forms characteristic of contemporary American poetry in the 1970s.

Although its poems have been disappearing from contemporary textbook anthologies, *Spoon River Anthology* is today as useful and appropriate an introduction to modern and contemporary poetry as one could hope to find. Its epitaphs anticipate the subgenre of confessional poetry that reached its apogee in American poetry in the 1950s and 1960s in the poems of Robert Lowell, Sylvia Plath, Anne Sexton, John Berryman, and others. The very unevenness of the *Anthology* gives it pedagogical advantages. The student can hear the literary diction and poetic inversions clashing against the homely American speech and conversational rhythms, can learn to distinguish the voice of the persona from the voice of the poet, and can decide the relative effectiveness of ironic implication and explicit commentary. The student of poetry and even the student poet can learn much besides from the complete *Anthology,* about the relationship of particular poems to the larger whole, the use of interrelated motifs, developing atttitudes and expectations. In short, one can learn something of the beginnings of the whole modern tradition of the poetic sequence: Hart Crane's *The Bridge* (1933), Eliot's *The Waste Land* (1922), Pound's *Cantos,* William Carlos Williams's *Paterson* (1963), Robert Lowell's *Life Studies* (1959) or *Notebook, 1967–1968,* and John Berryman's *Dream Songs* (1972).

For *Spoon River Anthology* was the catalyst of its age. Masters's great creative discovery was of the possibilities of the immune confession supported by the absolute critical objectivity of the grave, with a wide cast of characters of differing perspectives all bearing on a common life. His instinctual recognition of the passing of a way of life, illustrated in his own career from farm to village to metropolis, led him to preserve it in literature and to document the unchanging human imperatives—that we must love the land, man's only home, and that, in the words of another poet, we must love one another or die.

All his writing is instinct with that attachment to the land. In his last published book, *The Sangamon,* Masters reminded his readers of "the fable of Antaeus, the giant who could not be overcome unless his feet were taken from the earth" (83), and he applied the fable to Illinois farmers who sold their patrimony to move to the village and from the village to the city. They were the "sons of Antaeus" (84). At times he must have considered himself one of them, except that though his feet walked the city pavements, his heart remained at his grandparents' farm on the Illinois prairie, and his hopes for his country remained rooted in Thomas Jefferson's agrarian polity. Love of the land, love of country, and sexual love were to him inextricably bound together. The land implied freedom to grow and to prosper; the nation stood for political freedom, the right of every man to own and work his plot of earth; sexual freedom was simply a corollary of political freedom. He praised Jefferson and condemned Lincoln, he satirized the sexual repression of a Spoon River and exhibited himself as sexually liberated in *Across Spoon River* all with the same motive, to celebrate the land and himself as a free soul in a free country. In *Spoon River Anthology* and in his subsequent literary career which the success of *Spoon River* forced upon him, he was at once a realist and an optimist (pointing out remediable evils), a conservative patriot and a sexual rebel.

In many ways he was as he represented himself, a typical American only writ large, with greater energy, charisma, a more available genius ("brother god?") than most of us. In his writing of the repressed average, the dead of Spoon River, paradoxically he elevated himself and them to immortality and enlarged the scope of freedom for his readers. Like its archetype the *Greek Anthology, Spoon River Anthology,* although it speaks to a particular moment in American social history, will be continuously rediscovered. In its best poems, the characters though dead have the ring of life. They reveal to us the truths about ourselves that we did not know we knew. So Thomas Trevelyan in *Spoon River* discovered truths about himself from poems of the *Greek Anthology.* And Masters speaking through him discovers to us that we all become "singers," poets, even though "But once in our lives. . . ."

Notes and References

Chapter One

1. *Across Spoon River* (New York, 1936), p. 20; hereafter cited as *ASR*.
2. Kimball Flaccus, *Edgar Lee Masters: A Biographical and Critical Study* (Montpelier, 1954), p. 40. Flaccus refers to "my forthcoming biography of Edgar Lee Masters" (p. 3); it has not appeared.
3. A computer-printed booklet, prepared by Horace A. Howe, director of the Astro-Numeric Service, El Cerrito, California, and dated 7 November 1974, was prepared as "a tool to aid the professional astrologer in his delineation of the horoscope." A professional reading is contained on two cassette tapes (and eight pages of single-spaced typescript) made on 22 November 1974, by Frank Ianella, professional astrologer of Boulder, Colorado. These materials may be consulted at Norlin Library, University of Colorado, Boulder.
4. See Graham Hutton, *Midwest at Noon* (Chicago, 1946), quoted in Max Lerner, *America as a Civilization* (New York: Simon and Schuster, 1957), pp. 189–91.
5. "Genesis of Spoon River," *American Mercury* 28 (January 1933):41–42.
6. Masters, quoted in David Karsner, *Sixteen Authors to One* (New York, 1928), p. 130.
7. *The Sangamon* (New York, 1942), p. 55; Masters quoted in August Derleth, *Three Literary Men* (New York, 1963), p. 41.
8. *The Sangamon,* p. 116.
9. *The Living Thoughts of Ralph Waldo Emerson* (New York, 1940), pp. 14–15.

Chapter Two

1. John Cowper Powys, in a speech reported in the *New York Times,* 4 April 1915, sec. 5, pp. 7, 9. Masters's admiration for Whitman appears in many places, from an "Elegy" he wrote at Whitman's death in 1892 to his book *Whitman* forty-five years later.
2. *Mitch Miller* (New York, 1920), pp. 98, 99.
3. *Skeeters Kirby: A Novel* (New York, 1923), p. 16.

3. *Mark Twain: A Portrait* (New York, 1938), p. 22.

5. Ibid., pp. 2–26.

Chapter Three

1. See Max Putzel, "Masters's 'Maltravers': Ernest McGaffey," *American Literature* 31 (January 1960):491. Also see Putzel's suggestion that the name derives from Lord Lytton's *Ernest Maltravers* (1837), in Putzel's *The Man in the Mirror: William Marion Reedy and His Magazine* (Cambridge, Mass., 1963), p. 331, n. 1.

2. "Introduction to Chicago," *American Mercury* 31 (January 1934):57.

3. Opie Read, *I Remember* (New York, 1930), p. 93, quoted in Bernard Duffey, *The Chicago Renaissance in American Letters* (East Lansing, Mich., 1954), pp. 143–44.

4. Henry Adams, *The Education of Henry Adams* (New York: Random House, 1931), p. 343.

5. Reedy, quoted in Putzel, "Masters's 'Maltravers,' " p. 492.

6. Spiller et al., *Literary History of the United States* (New York: Macmillan, 1948), p. 1022.

7. Descriptive title of chapter 5 in table of contents to Darrow's *Story of My Life* (New York: Scribner's, 1932).

8. Darrow, *Farmington* (Chicago: McClurg, 1904), pp. 24, 9, 276.

9. Frank Kee Robinson, "The Edgar Lee Masters Collection at the University of Texas at Austin," (Ph.D. diss., University of Texas–Austin, 1969), pp. 53, 54.

10. Ellen Coyne Masters in William A. Sutton, "Sherwood Anderson's Second Wife," *Ball State University Forum* 7 (Spring 1966):43; Ellen C. Masters to John H. Wrenn, 17 November 1975.

Chapter Four

1. Dreiser to Mencken, 6 November 1924, in *Letters of Theodore Dreiser: A Selection,* 3 vols., ed. Robert H. Elias (Philadelphia: University of Pennsylvania, 1959), 2:432.

2. Putzel, *The Man in the Mirror,* p. 196.

3. Harriet Monroe, *A Poet's Life* (New York, 1938), p. 377; see also Eunice Tietjens, *The World at My Shoulder* (New York, 1938), p. 44.

4. Monroe, *Poet's Life,* p. 370.

5. Sandburg, *Mirror* 23 (27 November 1914):7.

6. "William Marion Reedy," *American Speech* 9 (April 1934):97.

7. "Genesis of Spoon River," p. 48.

8. "Introduction" to *The New Spoon River* (New York, 1968), pp. xix–xx.

9. T. K. Hedrick to Harry Hansen, in Hansen, *Midwest Portraits* (New York, 1923), p. 246.

10. Monroe, *Poet's Life,* p. 378.
11. Tietjens, *World,* pp. 43–44.
12. See manuscript material in the Eunice Tietjens Collection, Newberry Library, Chicago.
13. Reedy, in Putzel, *Man in the Mirror,* p. 198 and n. 16.
14. Tietjens, *World,* p. 43.
15. Putzel, *Man in the Mirror,* p. 215.
16. Quoted in Robinson, "The Edgar Lee Masters Collection," p. 65.

Chapter Five

1. Amy Lowell, *Tendencies in Modern American Poetry* (New York, 1917), p. 174.

Chapter Six

1. [Edward J. Wheeler], "Voices of the Living Poets," *Current Opinion* 57 (September 1914):204; [Alice Corbin Henderson], "Our Contemporaries," *Poetry* 5 (October 1914):378.
2. *Publisher's Weekly* 87 (1915):226–45; 89 (1916):239; cited in Max Putzel, *The Man in the Mirror,* pp. 211, 333.
3. *Literary Digest* 77 (12 May 1923):52–55.
4. *Reedy's Mirror* 23 (3 July 1914):6–7; 23 (31 July 1914):1–2; 23 (18 September 1914):1; 23 (20 November 1914):1–2; 23 (27 November 1914):7; 23 (18 December 1914):239; 23 (15 January 1915):4; 24 (2 April 1915):3; 24 (23 April 1915):3; 24 (21 May 1915):3, 10–11; *Current Opinion* 57 (September 1914):204; 58 (March 1915):201–2; 58 (April 1915):273; 58 (May 1915):356; *Poetry* 5 (October 1914):42–44; 5 (March 1915):280; *Chicago Evening Post,* 18 December 1914, p. 14; 30 April 1915, p. 12; *New York Times,* 4 April 1915, pp. 7, 9; *Chicago Daily Tribune,* 15 May 1915, p. 11; *Boston Evening Transcript,* 1 May 1915, sec. 3, p. 8; *New Republic* 2 (17 April 1915), supp., pp. 14–15; *Nation* 100 (27 May 1915):604; *Egoist* 2 (1 January 1915):11–12.
5. William Marion Reedy, "The Writer of Spoon River," *Reedy's Mirror* 23 (20 November 1914):1–2.
6. *New York Times Sunday Magazine,* 4 April 1915, pp. 7, 9.
7. *Mirror* 23 (27 November 1914):7, quoted in Putzel, *Man in the Mirror.*
8. [Edward J. Wheeler], "Voices of the Living Poets," *Current Opinion* 58 (March 1915):201.
9. Mencken Collection, Enoch Pratt Free Library, Baltimore.
10. Mencken, *Prejudices: First Series* (New York, 1919), pp. 88–89.
11. Pound to Monroe, 12 October 1914, in *Letters of Ezra Pound,* ed. D. D. Paige (New York: Harcourt Brace & World, 1950), p. 43. Quoted in Putzel, *Man in the Mirror,* pp. 2–9.

12. *Egoist* 2 (1 January 1915):11–12.

13. "Affirmations: Edgar Lee Masters," *Mirror* 24 (21 May 1915):10–12.

14. Pound, quoted in Noel Stock, *The Life of Ezra Pound* (New York: Random House, 1970), p. 169.

15. Braithwaite, "The Soul of Spoon River," p. 8; "Spoon River Anthology," *Forum* 55 (January 1916):118, 120.

16. Lawrence Gilman, "Moving Picture Poetry," *North American Review* 202 (August 1915):271–76.

17. Willard Huntington Wright, "Mr. Masters' 'Spoon River Anthology': A Criticism," *Forum* 55 (January 1916):109; *New York Times,* 2 January 1916, p. 2.

18. Ezra Pound, "Mr. Pound's Disgust," *Mirror* 24 (25 June 1915):26.

19. "What Is Poetry?" *Poetry,* September 1915, pp. 306–8.

20. Pound, quoted in Stock, *Life of Pound,* p. 208.

21. Dreiser to Mencken, in *Letters of Theodore Dreiser,* ed. Robert H. Elias (Philadelphia: University of Pennsylvania, 1959), pp. 170–71.

22. Tietjens, *World,* p. 45.

Chapter Seven

1. Tietjens, *World,* p. 45.

2. Monroe, *Poet's Life,* pp. 378, 375 respectively; Tietjens, *World,* p. 43.

3. Hardin Wallace Masters, *Edgar Lee Masters: A Biographical Sketchbook about a Famous American Author* (Rutherford, N.J., 1978), passim.

4. "Genesis of Spoon River," p. 55.

5. Lois Teal Hartley, "Edgar Lee Masters: A Critical Study" (Ph.D., diss., University of Illinois, 1949), p. 131.

6. Monroe, *Poetry* 24 (July 1924):204–8; 29 (March 1927):337, 339; 25 (February 1925):278; 29 (March 1927):337–38; 25 (February 1925):278, respectively.

7. Monroe, in *Poetry* 29 (March 1927):337.

8. See John T. Flanagan, *Edgar Lee Masters: The Spoon River Poet and His Critics* (Metuchen, N.J., 1974), pp. 137–39.

9. Tietjens, *World,* p. 21.

10. F. K. Robinson has collected vignettes numbered 1–6; see "Edgar Lee Masters Collection," pp. 176–83.

11. Robinson, "Edgar Lee Masters Collection," item 49, p. 62, indicates the early manuscript of *Domesday Book.*

12. See *Domesday Book* (New York, 1920), p. 155; hereafter cited as *DB;* and *Across Spoon River,* p. 358.

13. Stuart Pratt Sherman, "Poetic Personalities," *Yale Review* 10 (April 1921):636; Padraic Colum, "A Man of Lawe's Tale," *New Republic* 25 (29 December 1920):148.

14. Hardin Masters, *Edgar Lee Masters,* p. 62.

15. Sonnet dated 4 March 1928 in folder 12, Tietjens Collection, Newberry Library, Chicago.

Chapter Eight

1. See the final chapter of *Children of the Market Place* (New York, 1922) and discussion at the end of the present chapter.

2. Letters dated Chicago 1950, Dorothy Dow Collection, Newberry Library, Chicago.

3. Another account, by a woman friend of his later years, is Gertrude Claytor, "Edgar Lee Masters in the Chelsea Years," *Princeton University Library Chronicle* 14 (Autumn 1952):1–29. Two important accounts already referred to are Hardin Masters's recent memoir and Alice Davis's unpublished "Evenings with Edgar." See also Dale Kramer, *Chicago Renaissance* (New York, 1966), pp. 358–59. The fullest, most affectionate published treatment of Masters is the recent reminiscence by his son Hilary Masters, *Last Stands* (Boston: David R. Godine, 1982).

4. From a transcript made by Mrs. Fern Nance Pond of Masters's letter to her of 4 August 1938, quoted by Hartley, "Edgar Lee Masters," p. 241.

5. *Children of the Market Place,* p. 68.

Chapter Nine

1. See Hartley, "Edgar Lee Masters," pp. 247–48; Hartley quotes from her correspondence with Ellen Coyne Masters.

2. *Jack Kelso, A Dramatic Poem* (New York: 1928), p. 124.

3. Edgar Lee Masters, Miscellaneous Papers, Princeton University Library, this appears to be an original carbon-copy used as a proof sheet for a five-page review entitled "A Definitive Biography."

4. "Genesis of Spoon River," p. 55.

5. Robinson, "Edgar Lee Masters Collection," p. 63.

6. *Vachel Lindsay, A Poet in America* (New York, 1935), p. 192.

7. *Whitman* (New York, 1937), pp. 326–27.

8. *The Living Thoughts of Ralph Waldo Emerson,* p. 39.

9. *Mark Twain,* p. 102.

Chapter Ten

1. Johann Wolfgang von Goethe, quoted in Randall Jarrell, *Poetry and the Age* (New York: Noonday Press, 1972), pp. 140–41.

2. Monroe, *Poet's Life,* pp. 380–81.

3. "Letter," *New York Evening Post Literary Review* 16 (October 1926):23.

4. Portraits that contain recognizable Masters biography are, from the "Fifth Garland" (24 July 1914), "Francis Turner," "John Horace Burleson," "Henry Layton"; from the "Sixth Garland" (7 August), "Petit, the Poet"; from the "Tenth Garland" (4 September), "Daniel M'Cumber" and "Georgine Sand Miner," "Hamilton Greeve," "Immanuel Ehrenhardt"; from the "Fourteenth Garland" (2 October), "Le Roy Goldman"; from the "Eighteenth Garland" (30 October), "Thomas Trevelyan"; then "Elijah Browning" and "Herbert Marshall" (13 November), "Dillard Sissman" (20 November), "Hamlet Micure" (4 December), "Alfred Moir" (25 December), "Ezra Bartlett" (1 January 1915), "Webster Ford" (15 January), followed by "Paul McNeely," "Voltair Johnson," and "Jonathan Houghton" added to the second edition.

5. Hardin Masters, *Edgar Lee Masters,* p. 52.

6. Willard Thorpe, in Robert E. Spiller, et al, *Literary History of the United States* (New York: Macmillan, 1949), p. 1180.

7. Walter Havighurst, *The Heartland* (New York: Harper, 1956), p. 332.

8. John Dos Passos, "Book Reviews," *Harvard Monthly* 62 (May 1916):89.

Selected Bibliography

PRIMARY SOURCES

1. Poetry

Along the Illinois. Prairie City, Ill.: James A. Decker, 1942.

[Dexter Wallace, pseud.] *The Blood of the Prophets*. Chicago: Rooks Press, 1905.

A Book of Verses. Chicago: Way and Williams, 1898.

Domesday Book. New York: Macmillan, 1920.

Dramatic Duologues, Four Short Plays in Verse. New York: Samuel French, 1934.

The Fate of the Jury, An Epilogue to Domesday Book. New York: D. Appleton, 1929.

Gettysburg, Manila, Ácoma. New York: Liveright, 1930.

Godbey, A Dramatic Poem. New York: Dodd, Mead, 1931.

The Golden Fleece of California. New York: Farrar and Rinehart, 1936.

The Great Valley. New York: Macmillan, 1916.

Illinois Poems. Prairie City, Ill.: James A. Decker, 1941.

Invisible Landscapes. New York: Macmillan, 1935.

Jack Kelso, A Dramatic Poem. New York: D. Appleton, 1928.

Lee, A Dramatic Poem. New York: Macmillan, 1926.

Lichee Nuts. New York: Liveright, 1930.

More People. New York: D. Appleton-Century, 1939.

The New Spoon River. New York: Boni and Liveright, 1924.

The New World. New York: D. Appleton-Century, 1937.

The Open Sea. New York: Macmillan, 1921.

Poems of People. New York: D. Appleton-Century, 1936.

Posthumous Poems of Edgar Lee Masters. Edited by Frank Kee Robinson. Preface by Padraic Colum. Austin: University of Texas, Humanities Research Center, 1969.

Richmond, A Dramatic Poem. New York: Samuel French, 1934.

Selected Poems. New York: Macmillan, 1925.

The Serpent in the Wilderness. New York: Sheldon Dick, 1933.

Songs and Satires. New York: Macmillan, 1916.

[Webster Ford, pseud.] *Songs and Sonnets*. Chicago: Rooks Press, 1910.

[Webster Ford, pseud.] *Songs and Sonnets, Second Series*. Chicago: Rooks
    Press, 1912.
Spoon River Anthology. New York: Macmillan, 1915.
Spoon River Anthology. Introduction by Edgar Lee Masters and illustrations
    by Boardman Robinson. New York: Limited Editions Club, 1942.
Spoon River Anthology. New edition with new poems. New York: Mac-
    millan, 1916.
Starved Rock. New York: Macmillan, 1919.
Toward the Gulf. New York: Macmillan, 1918.

2. Novels
Children of the Market Place. New York: Macmillan, 1922.
Kit O'Brien. New York: Boni and Liveright, 1927.
Mirage. New York: Boni and Liveright, 1924.
Mitch Miller. Illustrated by John Sloan. New York: Macmillan, 1920.
The Nuptial Flight. New York: Boni and Liveright, 1923.
Skeeters Kirby, A Novel. New York: Macmillan, 1923.
The Tide of Time. New York: Farrar and Rinehart, 1937.

3. Biography
Levy Mayer and the New Industrial Era. New Haven: Yale University Press,
    1927.
Lincoln: The Man of the People. New York: Dodd, Mead, 1931.
Mark Twain, A Portrait. New York: Charles Scribner's Sons, 1938.
Vachel Lindsay, A Poet in America. New York: Charles Scribner's Sons,
    1935.
Whitman. New York: Charles Scribner's Sons, 1937.

4. Autobiography
Across Spoon River, An Autobiography. New York: Farrar and Rinehart, 1936.

5. Plays
Althea, A Play in Four Acts. Chicago: Rooks Press, 1907.
The Bread of Idleness, A Play in Four Acts. Chicago: Rooks Press, 1911.
Eileen, A Play in Three Acts. Chicago: Rooks Press, 1910.
The Leaves of the Tree, A Play. Chicago: Rooks Press, 1909.
The Locket, A Play in Three Acts. Chicago: Rooks Press, 1910.
Maximilian. A Play in Five Acts. Boston: Richard G. Badger, 1902.
The Trifler, A Play. Chicago: Rooks Press, 1908.

6. Nonfiction
The Living Thoughts of Ralph Waldo Emerson. Edited, with introduction,
    by Masters. New York: David McKay, 1940.

The New Star Chamber and Other Essays. Chicago: Hammersmark Publishing Company, 1904.

The Sangamon. New York: Farrar and Rinehart, 1942.

The Tale of Chicago. New York: G. P. Putman's Sons, 1933.

7. Periodical contributions

"Abe Lincoln's New Salem." *Rotarian* 64 (February 1944):32–33.

"The American Background." *Nation* 121 (26 August 1925):226–29.

"The Artist Revolts." *Poetry* 22 (July 1923):206–9.

"A Call for Secession." *American Mercury* 27 (November 1932):373–74.

"Chicago, Yesterday, To-Day and To-Morrow." *Century Magazine* 116 (July 1928):283–94.

"The Christian Statesman." *American Mercury* 3 (December 1924):385–98.

"A Correction." *Poetry* 12 (September 1918):345.

"Days in the Lincoln Country." *Journal of the Illinois State Historical Society* 18 (January 1926):779–92.

"A Democrat Looks at His Party." *American Mercury* 25 (January 1932):82–90.

"Demos the Despot." *New Republic* 17 (25 January 1919):374–75.

"Dreiser at Spoon River." *Esquire* 11 (May 1939):66ff.

"Edgar Lee Masters." In *Portraits and Self-Portraits*, edited by Georges Schreiber. Boston: Houghton Mifflin, 1936, pp. 91–94.

"Every Word Is Intentional." *Poetry* 52 (September 1938):356–59.

"Father Mallory." *Commonweal* 8 (14 December 1927):811–13.

"Four Americans." *American Mercury* 38 (July 1936):372–75.

"The Genesis of Spoon River." *American Mercury* 28 (January 1933):38–55.

"Grover Cleveland." *American Mercury* 8 (August 1926):385–97.

"Harriet Monroe." *Poetry* 69 (December 1936):153.

"Histories of the American Mind." *American Mercury* 35 (July 1935):341–45.

"How to Debunk Abraham Lincoln." *American Mercury* 37 (February 1936):241–44.

"I Call Her Dorcas." *Rotarian* 62 (May 1943):8–10, 60.

"In Search of a Better Religion." *McNaught's Monthly* 5 (June–July 1926):163–67, 12–15.

"Introduction to Chicago." *American Mercury* 31 (January 1934):49–59.

"James Whitcomb Riley." *Century Magazine* 114 (October 1927):704–15.

"John Cowper Powys." *Reedy's Mirror* 25 (5 May 1916):303.

"John Peter Altgeld." *American Mercury* 4 (February 1925):161ff.

"Labor Troubles in Illinois." *New Republic* 3 (19 June 1915):178–79.

"Letter." *New York Evening Post Literary Review*, 16 October 1926, p. 23.

"Letter to Harriet Monroe." *Poetry* 158 (June 1936):175–77.
"Literary Boss of the Middle West." *American Mercury* 34 (April 1935):450–55.
"Machine Age Comes to Spoon River." *Today* 1 (14 April 1934):8–9.
"Mark Twain: Son of the Frontier." *American Mercury* 36 (September 1935):67–74.
"Mars Has Descended." *Poetry* 10 (May 1917):88–92.
"M[ary] F[isher]'s *Kirstie.*" *Mirror* 21 (7 November 1912):6.
"Miss Monroe's 'You and I.' " *Reedy's Mirror* 23 (22 January 1915):5–6.
"New Hope Meeting House." *University Review* 4 (Winter 1937):95–96.
"The Poetry Revival of 1914." *American Mercury* 26 (July 1932):272–80.
"The Return." *Poetry* 22 (September 1923):291–303.
"A 'Spoon River' Boost." *Poetry* 6 (May 1915):103.
"Stephen A. Douglas." *American Mercury* 22 (January 1931):11–23.
"Suggestions from Dr. Chubb." *Poetry* 32 (June 1928):173–74.
"To the People of Petersburg and Menard County." *University Review* 3 (Winter 1936):107–8.
"The Tragedy of Vachel Lindsay." *American Mercury* 29 (July 1933):357–69.
"Vachel Lindsay." *Bookman* 64 (October 1926):156–60.
"Vachel Lindsay and America." *Saturday Review of Literature* 12 (10 August 1935):3–4, 15.
"The War Between the States and the New Era." *Watson's Magazine* 6 (November–December 1906):56–61, 249–56.
"The Way of Art Young." *Bookman* 68 (January 1929):595–96.
"What Is Great Poetry?" *Poetry* 26 (September 1925):349–51.
"What Is Poetry?" *Poetry* 26 (September 1915):306–8.
"William Marion Reedy." *American Speech* 9 (April 1934):96–98.
"*You and I* by Harriet Monroe." *Poetry* 5 (January 1915):188–91.

8. Unpublished plays in manuscript, Edgar Lee Masters Collection at the University of Texas at Austin
"Alum, A Play." 1919.
"Antony and Cleopatra, A Drama." 1935.
"Benedict Arnold, A Play." 1893.
"Far Horizons." 1947?
"House in the Wood." 1928.
"Lilah, A Play." 1913 or earlier?
"Love and the Law, A Play." 1913 or earlier?
"Manuscript of a Novel, A Play." 1922?
"Moroni, A Play." 1934. Performed 18–22 August 1936 at Mohawk Drama festival (Schenectady, New York), directed by Charles Coburn.
"Newport, A Play." 1908?

"New Salem, A Play." 1909?
"Separate Maintenance, A Play." 1923?
"Titanomachia, A Play." 1933?
"Widow La Rue, A Play." 1932.
"Wood Alcohol, A Play." 1929.

9. Lectures, pamphlets, and tracts
"Browning as a Philosopher." Paper delivered to Chicago Literary Club,
    18 November 1912.
"The Constitution and Our Insular Possessions." 1900.
Theodore Dreiser: America's Foremost Novelist. 1917. Coauthor.

10. Manuscript collections
Austin. University of Texas, Edgar Lee Masters Collection. Manuscripts,
    miscellaneous papers, unpublished work. Described by Frank Kee
    Robinson (see below).
Chicago. Newberry Library. Dorothy Dow Collection. Correspondence,
    with Dow's "Edgar Lee Masters: An Introduction to Some Letters."
Chicago. Newberry Library. Eunice Tietjens Collection. Correspondence.
Chicago. Newberry Library. Masters Papers. Miscellaneous items includ-
    ing letters and unpublished verse.
Philadelphia. University of Pennsylvania Library. Dreiser Collection.
    Correspondence.
Providence, R.I. Brown University. Hilary Masters Collection.

SECONDARY SOURCES

1. Bibliographies
Flanagan, John T. *Edgar Lee Masters: The Spoon River Poet and His Critics.*
    Metuchen, N.J.: Scarecrow Press, 1974. A painstakingly annotated
    catalog of the major reviews of Masters's work, arranged chronolog-
    ically, as well as Masters's inclusions in histories and anthologies.
Robinson, Frank Kee. "The Edgar Lee Masters Collection at the Uni-
    versity of Texas at Austin: A Critical, Bibliographical, and Textual
    Study." *Library Chronicle of the University of Texas* 8 (Spring 1968):42–
    49. A listing and description of the Masters Collection at Texas. A
    more complete version is Robinson's 1969 dissertation, with the same
    title.

2. Books, parts of books, and articles

Barnstone, Willis. Introduction to *The New Spoon River*. New York: Macmillan, 1968. The most thorough analysis of Masters's debt to the *Greek Anthology*.

Claytor, Gertrude. "Edgar Lee Masters in the Chelsea Years." *Princeton University Chronicle* 14 (Autumn 1952):1–29. Mrs. Claytor's sketch gives an informal portrait of the poet as seen by his friend and frequent hostess.

Duffey, Bernard. *The Chicago Renaissance in American Letters*. East Lansing: Michigan State College Press, 1954. Useful for the intellectual and social ambience of Chicago in the period following the Chicago Exposition of 1903; emphasizes political liberalism.

Flaccus, Kimball. *Edgar Lee Masters: A Biographical and Critical Study*. Montpelier: Vermont Historical Society, 1954. An abridged form of Flaccus's 1952 doctoral dissertation, reprinted from "The Vermont Background of Edgar Lee Masters," *Vermont History* 22 (1954, entire):3–9, 92–98, 172–78, 254–63; 23 (January 1955):16–24. Useful on Masters's mother, Emma Masters.

Hansen, Harry. *Midwest Portraits*. New York: Harcourt, Brace, 1923. Useful in any effort to define the Midwest character; with occasional nuggets not found elsewhere, on Masters and other recollected acquaintances.

Hartley, Lois Teal. "The Early Plays of Edgar Lee Masters." *Ball State University Forum* 7 (Spring 1966):26–38. Valuable more for the considered judgments, largely unfavorable, of a perceptive critic than for the importance of the plays.

Karsner, David. *Sixteen Authors to One*. New York: Louis Capeland, 1928. Gives Masters's view—somewhat rationalized after the fact—of his parents' contribution to the *Anthology*.

Kramer, Dale. *Chicago Renaissance, The Literary Life of the Midwest 1900–1930*. New York: Appleton-Century, 1966. A readable, well researched update of material covered earlier, but less thoroughly, by Bernard Duffey.

Lowell, Amy. *Tendencies in Modern American Poetry*. New York: Macmillan, 1919. Interesting as a contemporary evaluation by an influential poet-critic (perhaps the only one to compare Masters to the Swedish playwright and novelist Arthur Strindberg).

Masters, Hardin Wallace. *Edgar Lee Masters: A Biographical Sketchbook About a Famous American Author*. Rutherford, N.J.: Fairleigh Dickinson University Press, 1978. A rambling but informative reminiscence by the poet's son by his first marriage, written in the son's eighth decade; includes photographs.

————. *Edgar Lee Masters: A Centenary Memoir-Anthology.* New York: Poetry Society of America, 1972. A first venture in recollecting the Masters past; less complete than the *Sketchbook.*

Mencken, Henry Lewis. *Prejudices: First Series.* New York: A. A. Knopf, 1919, pp. 88–89. Contains some devastating criticism of Masters (and others) by a perceptive critic.

Monroe, Harriet. *A Poet's Life.* New York: Macmillan, 1938. Prejudiced in favor of Masters as a Chicago poet, but informative and judicious at the same time—important as the views of the editor of *Poetry* magazine, at the center of the Chicago renaissance.

Pound, Ezra. "Affirmations: Edgar Lee Masters." *Reedy's Mirror* 24 (21 May 1915):10–12. Important both in its astute criticism of Spoon River poems and as a marker in the development of Pound's critical positions.

————. "Mr. Pound's Disgust." *Reedy's Mirror* 24 (25 June 1915):26. Attacks the conservative critics of *Spoon River.*

————. "Webster Ford." *Egoist* 2 (1 January 1915):11–12. Pound's enthusiastic discovery of a true American poet.

Putzel, Max. *The Man in the Mirror: William Marion Reedy and His Magazine.* Cambridge: Harvard University Press, 1963. Carefully researched biography of Masters's literary mentor and closest friend.

————. "Masters's 'Maltravers' " Ernest McGaffey." *American Literature* 31 (January 1960):491–93. Identifies Masters's close friend, who introduced him to Reedy.

Tietjens, Eunice. *The World at My Shoulder.* New York: Macmillan, 1938. An editor of *Poetry*, a close friend of Masters, comments on his personality and on the creation of *Spoon River Anthology.*

Wrenn, John H., and **Wrenn, Margaret M.** " 'T.M.': The Forgotten Muse of Sherwood Anderson and Edgar Lee Masters." In *Sherwood Anderson: Centennial Studies.* Troy: N.Y.: Whitsun Publishing Co., 1976, pp. 175–84. A study of Tennessee Mitchell's role in the creation of the major works of Masters *(Spoon River)* and Anderson *(Winesburg, Ohio).*

3. Dissertation

Hartley, Lois Teal. "Edgar Lee Masters: A Critical Study." Ph.D. dissertation, University of Illinois, 1949. The pioneering book-length study of Masters.

Index

Adams, Henry, 24
Album of Authors, 63, 64, 102
Altgeld, John Peter, 28, 29; *Our Penal Code and Its Victims*, 29
Anderson, Sherwood, 18, 30, 120, 121; *Winesburg Ohio*, 30, 71, 120
Armstrong, John, 35, 36
Astrology, 1–3, 119
Atherton, Lewd, 118; *See also* Ford, Webster

Baum, Bertha, 68, 70, 71, 75
Bellamy, Edward: *Looking Backward*, 20
Berryman, John: *Dream Songs*, 122
Beveridge, Albert: *Life of Abraham Lincoln*, 104
Bhagavad-gita, 74
Boston Evening Transcript, 59
Braithwaite, W. S., 61
Browning, Robert, 62, 66; *Ring and the Book, The*, 15, 64, 74
Bryan, William Jennings, 19, 27, 29, 101, 102, 106
Bryant, William Cullen, 67

Cather, Willa: *O Pioneers*, 66
Catholic Anthology, 61, 120; *See also* Pound, Ezra
Chaucer, Geoffrey, 71, 105, 106

Chicago, 6, 9, *21–29*, 35, 38, 39, 54, 64, 70, 71, 88, 101, 112
Chicago Chronicle, 22, 27, 28
Chicago Evening Post, 59
Chicago Inter-Ocean, 22
Chicago Press Club, 23–25
Chicago Record, 11
Chicago Tribune, 59
Claytor, Mrs. Gertrude, 105
Colliers, 60
Colum, Padraic, 76
Columbian Exposition, 12, 22, 23, 25
Comstock, Anthony: Comstock Laws, Comstockery, 15, 34, 36, 52, 71
Crabbe, George, 63, 64
Crane, Hart: *The Bridge*, 122
Crane, Stephen: *Maggie*, 27; *Red Badge of Courage, The*, 27
Current Opinion, 58, 59; Wheeler, Edward J.: of *Spoon River Anthology*, 58

Darrow, Clarence, 14, 20, 22, 29, 31, 77, 88, 89; *Farmington*, 29, 30; *Story of My Life, The*, 29
Darwin, Charles, 102; *Origin of the Species*, 14
Davis, Alice, 92, 100, 114

Derleth, August: *Selected Poems,* 121

Dial, The, 62

Dickinson, Emily, 56

Dos Passos, John: *U.S.A.,* 120, 121

Douglas, Stephen A., 98, 101, 109; *See also* Masters, E. L.: *Children of the Market Place*

Dow, Dorothy: "Edgar Lee Masters . . .," 93

Dreiser, Theodore, 14, 15, 18, 22, 34–36, 40, 41, 59, 60, 66, 70, 93, 109, 113, 116; *Bulwark, The,* 35; *Financier, The,* 34; *Sister Carrie,* 19, 34, 36, 37, 66; *Titan, The,* 34, 35

Eggleston, Edward, 16, 21; *Hoosier Schoolmaster, The,* 16

Egoist, The, 59

Eliot, T. S., 58, 120; *Prufrock . . . ,* 71; *Waste Land, The,* 116, 120, 122

Emerson, Ralph Waldo, 11, 65, 70, 102, 105, 108; "Hamatreya," 65; *Representative Men,* 102

Epilogue, 46, 77, 97, 113, 114, 117

Etter, Dave: *Go Read the River,* 122

Faulkner, William, 30, 121

Field, Eugene, 11; "Sharps and Flats," 19

Fisher, Mary, 11, 12, 49, 102, 113

FitzGerald, Edward: *Rubaiyat of Omar Khayyam,* 15

Flaccus, Kimball, 2

Ford, Webster, 32, 39, 41, 47, 56, 60, 61, 68, 137; *See also* Atherton, Lewd

Forum, 62

Freud, Sigmund, 92

Frost, Robert, 58; *Mountain Interval,* 71; *North of Boston,* 71

Gale, Zona: *Miss Lulu Bett,* 121

Garland, Hamlin, 21, 60; *Main Travelled Roads,* 19

George, Henry: *Progress and Poverty,* 18, 20

George, Margaret Gilman, 11, 12, 56, 62, 85, 86, 93, 96, 98, 113

Gettysburg Address, 105

Gilbert, W. S.: *Pinafore,* 65

Gilman, Lawrence: "Moving Picture Poetry," 61

Goethe, Johann Wolfgang von, 61, 98, 101, 105, 114, 115

Gray, Thomas, 66

Greek Anthology, The, 31, 36, 37, 40, 63, 123

Hardy, Thomas: "Ah, Are You Digging on My Grave?" 65

Hartley, Lois T., 72

Havighurst, Walter: *The Heartland: Ohio, Indiana, Illinois,* 120

Hay, John: *Pike County Ballads,* 16

Heartland, Poets of the Midwest: Bly, Robert, 122; Brooks, Gwendolyn, 122; Stafford, William, 122; Tate, James, 122; Wright, James, 122

Helen Haire Levinson Prize, 59

Homer, 80

Housman, A. E., 15; "Night Is Freezing Fast, The," 65; "Is My Team Plowing?" 15, 65; *Shropshire Lad, A,* 15, 27, 65

Howe, E. W., 19, 121; *Anthology of Another Town, The,* 121; *Story of a Country Town, The,* 19

Howells, William D., 21

Irwin, Orvis, 62

Jackson, Andrew, 98, 110
Jeffers, Robinson, 121
Jefferson, Thomas, 98, 101, 102,
   104, 105, 107, 108, 110, 114,
   123
Jeffersonian Magazine, 27
Jenkins, Helen, 28

Keats, John, 64
Kipling, Rudyard, 66
Kirkland, Joseph: *Zury,* 19
Knox College, 13, 39, 45, 52,
   80, 96

Lawrence, D. H.: "The Snake,"
   73
Lewis, Sinclair, 30, 120; *Main
   Street,* 71, 121; *Our Mr. Wrenn,*
   71
Lewistown, 4–6, 8, 9, 14, 18,
   22, 25, 26, 28, 41, 49, 56,
   63, 66, 74, 87, 92, 95, 110,
   112, 115
Lincoln, Abraham, 98, 101, *103–
   105,* 106, 109, 110, 123; *See
   also* Masters, E. L.: *Lincoln: The
   Man*
Lindsay, Vachel, 18, 58, 60, 70,
   109; *See also* Masters, E. L.:
   Vachel Lindsay; The Congo, 71
Literary Digest, 59
Little Review, 62
Loomis, Roger Sherman, 62
Lowell, Amy, 117; *Sword Blades
   and Poppy Seeds,* 71; *Tendencies in
   Modern American Poetry,* 54, 60
Lowell, Robert, 122; *Life Studies,*
   121, 122; *Notebook,* 122

McGaffey, Ernest, 22, 23, 25,
   26, 31, 34, 40, 86, 113
McGovern, John, 22
March, William: *Company K,* 121
Marshall, John, 87
Masefield, John: *The Everlasting
   Mercy,* 65
Masters, Alexander, 3, 4, 10, 16,
   49
Masters, Edgar Lee:

WORKS: PLAYS
Alum, 103
Benedict Arnold, 103
Manuscript of a Novel, 103
Maximilian, 26, 103
Trifler, The, 96

POETRY, BOOKS
Acoma, 104
Along the Illinois, 74, 110
Book of Verses, A, 16, 26, 28
Fate of the Jury, The, 15, 30,
   55, 70, 76–81
Golden Fleece of California, The,
   80
Gettysburg, 104
Great Valley, The, 2, 5, 24, 61,
   68, 71, 116
Illinois Poems, 74, 110
Invisible Landscapes, 73
Jack Kelso, A Dramatic Poem,
   103, 105
Lee: A Dramatic Poem, 103
Lichee Nuts, 47, 72, 117, 118
Manila, 104
More People, 73, 103, 108, 110
New Spoon River, The, 7, 18,
   47, 66, 67, 72, 117
New World, The, 70, 71, 108
Open Sea, The, 33, 44, 71
Poems of People, 73, 107, 108,
   110
Selected Poems, 41, 72

Serpent in the Wilderness, The, 73
Songs and Satires, 1, 44, 61, 68, 69, 71, 110
Songs and Sonnets, 41, 64, 88, 110, 116
Songs and Sonnets, Second Series, 41, 61, 64
Spoon River Anthology, 1, 3, 15, 16, 20, 22, 26, 28–32, 35–37, 39–43, 45–67, 68–78, 81, 88, 89, 95, 101, 103–106, 110–13, 115–19, 121–23
Starved Rock, 71

POETRY, INDIVIDUAL POEMS
"Aaron Hatfield," 66
"A.D. Blood," 21, 48, 51
"Adam Weirauch," 66
"Albert Thurston," 66
"Alfred Moir," 67
"Amanda Barker," 45, 46,
"Anne Rutledge," 57, 101
"Anson Harms," 73
"Anthony Findlay," 66
"Ballade of Ultimate Shame. . . ," 32
"Barry Holden," 66
"Beethoven's Ninth Symphony and the King Cobra," 73
"Benjamin Pantier," 65
"Bill Dill," 73
"Blind Jack," 48
" 'Butch' Weldy," 48
"Caroline Branson," 47
"Cassius," 45, 46
"Chase Henry," 45, 46
"Circuit Judge, The," 21, 78
"Confucius and Tsze-Lû," 73
"Conrad Siever," 65
"Cooney Potter," 47
"Daisy Frazier," 54
"Davis Matlock," 56

"Death of William Marion Reedy, The," 44
"Dr. Atherton," 24
"Doc Hill," 61
"Dr. Meyers," 48, 50
"Dr. Siegrfied Iseman," 47
"Edith Bell," 18
"Editor Whedon," 21, 50
"Elijah Browning," 66
"Elmer Chubb," 24
"Else Wertman," 19
"Emily Sparks," 49, 55, 57, 66
"Epilogue," 46, 47
"Fate of a Tribune," 103
"Fiddler Jones," 20, 56
"Fletcher McGee," 51
"Flossie Cabanis," 66
"Flowers of Illinois," 110
"George Trimble," 19
"Gustav Richter," 47, 67
"Hamlet Micure," 4, 49, 66
"Hannah Armstrong," 57
"Hare Drummer," 15, 65
"Hill, The," 45, 46, 52, 61, 63, 66
"Hod Putt," 20, 21, 45, 46, 48, 118
"Hortense Robbins," 120, 121
"House Where Mark Twain Was Born, The," 108
" 'Indignation' Jones," 51
"Ippolit Konovaloff," 65
"John Hancock Otis," 21
"John Wasson," 28, 49, 51, 57
"Johnnie Sayre," 49
"Jonathan Houghton," 66
"Jonathan Swift Somers," 50
"Judge Somers," 48
"Kinsey Keene," 47
"Launcelot and Elaine," 116
"LeRoy Goldman," 47
"Little Billy," 11
"Little Paul," 49

"Lucinda Matlock," 20, 56, 57, 121
"Lucius Atherton," 54
"Lute Puckett," 24
"Many Soldiers," 48, 55, 57
"Marie Bateson," 57
"Minerva Jones," 48, 50
"Mrs. Charles Bliss," 21
"Mrs. Meyers," 48
"Neanderthal," 4
"Nellie Clark," 47
"Nicholas Bindle," 48
"Ollie McGee," 45, 46, 48, 51
"Peerless Leader, The," 19
"Petit, the Poet," 51, 63
"Priam Finish," 67
"Rebecca Wasson," 20, 49, 56, 57
"Robert Southey Burke," 21
"Rutherford McDowell," 57
"Sarah Brown," 57
"Search, The," 2
"Searcy Foote," 66
"Serepta Mason," 45, 46, 51
"Silence," 69, 116
"Sexsmith the Dentist," 47
"Spooniad, The," 46, 50, 65, 77
"Star, The," 1, 4
"Theodore the Poet," 37, 66
"Thomas Rhodes," 21, 49, 53
"To a Spirochaeta," 24
"Town Marshall, The," 48
"Ulysses," 33
"Unknown, The," 45, 46, 48
"Village Atheist, The," 48, 56
"Vision, The," 69
"Webster Ford," 47, 56, 68
"William and Emily," 48, 55, 66
"William H. Herndon," 57
"William Marion Reedy," 44
"William Metcalf," 73

PROSE, BOOKS
Across Spoon River, 1, 2, 4, 8, 17, 22, 23, 29, 32, 34, 35, 39, 40, 41, 56, 58, 62, 64, 68, 74–76, 79–81, 85, 86, 88, 92–94, 96, 99, 105, 108, *112–15*, 123
Children of the Market Place, 85, 93, *98–101*, 106
Domesday Book, 7, 15, 30, 64, 74–79, 81, 88, 117–21
Living Thoughts of Ralph Waldo Emerson, The, 65, *102–103*, 108
Kit O'Brien, 81, *83–85*, 98
Levy Mayer and the New Industrial Revolution, 103
Lincoln: The Man of the People, 18, 70, 101, *104–105*, 106
Mark Twain, 2, 17, *108–109*
Mirage, 30, 79, 83, 88–94
Mitch Miller, 3, 70, 75, *81–85*, 101
New Star Chamber, The, 27, 28, 29
Nuptial Flight, The, 4, 7, 8, 90, *93–96*
Sangamon, The, 3, 35, 36, 73, *109–110*, 123
Skeeters Kirby, 17, 56, 79, 81, 83, *85–89*, 93, 94, 96, 103
Tale of Chicago, The, 112
Tide of Time, The, 1, 15, 74, 81, 93, *95–99*, 108
Vachel Lindsay, 18, 70, *106–107*, 112
Whitman, 12, 55, 105, *108*, 114

PROSE, ESSAYS
"Browning as a Philosopher," 15, 75

"Genesis of Spoon River, The,"
6, 31, 36, 41, *63–64*, 70,
81, 102
"Literary Boss of the Middle
West," 43
"What Is Poetry?" 63

Masters, Ellen Coyne, 32, 78, 92,
94, 100
Masters, Emma, 3, 7, 8, 13, 18,
22, 25, 41, 90, 93, 96, 98,
106
Masters, Hardin (father), 2, 7,
12–14, 25, 27, 29, 31, 82,
84, 94, 99; *See also* Masters,
E. L.: *The Tide of Time*
Masters, Hardin (son), 78; "Bio-
graphical Sketchbook," 70
Masters, Helen Jenkins, 30–
32,70, 86–88, 96, 108
Masters, Hilary, 78, 89
Masters, Lucinda, 10, 22, 25, 27,
29, 31–33, 49, 56, 87, 92,
94, 96, 110, 113
Masters, Madeline (Madeline
Stone), 8, 10, 25, 94, 98
Masters, Mary, 3, 4
Masters, Squire Davis, 55, 56,
93, 94, 96, 98, 99, 109, 110
Masters, Thomas Davis, 11, 94
Mencken, H. L., 37, 60, 70,
113, 116; *American Mercury,*
112; *Prejudices: First Series,* 60,
65; *Smart Set, The,* 35, 60
Meyer, Abraham, 103
Mill, John Stuart: *On Liberty,* 14
Miller, Mitch, 3, 4, 16, 40, 44,
49, 50, 86, 98, 110; *See also*
Masters, E. L.: *Mitch Miller*
Mitchell, Tennessee, 22, *31–34,*
37, 40, 41, 55, 75, 78, 79,
86, 87, 88, 95, 96
Monroe, Harriet, 38, 39, 41, 67–
69, 72, 113; *See also Poetry*

Poet's Life, A, 38, 39, 41, 60,
116
Moody, Mrs. William Vaughn,
63

Nation, The, 59
New Republic, The, 59
*New York Evening Post Literary Re-
view,* 116
New York Times, 59, 60, 62

Paine, Thomas: *Common Sense,* 119
Petersburg, 4, 5, 8, 9, 14, 18,
22, 25, 27, 32, 33, 35, 41,
43, 49, 74, 83, 92, 93, 95,
101, 103, 108–110, 115
Phillips, William L., 32
Plath, Sylvia, 122
Plato, 102
Plotinus, 102
Poe, Edgar Allen, 18, 81, 105
Poetry, 38, 39, 41, 45, 58, 59,
72
Pound, Ezra, 38, 45, 58, 60–63,
116, 120; *Cantos,* 122; *Catholic
Anthology,* 61, 120
Powys, John Cowper, 37, 59, 67,
71, 105, 113
Prassel, Jake, 47, 70
Publisher's Weekly, 58, 59
Putzel, Max, 37, 43

Reedy, William Marion, 22, 34,
36, 40–44, 46, 47, 58–60,
77, 80, 87–89, 98, 113, 115,
116, 118; *Reedy's Mirror,* 22,
26, 34, 36–43, 58, 59, 61,
62, 68, 70
Reid, Opie, 23
Robinson, Edwin Arlington, 16,
30, 61, 62, 64, 73; *Man
Against the Sky, The,* 71; *Town
Down the River, The,* 64
Roosevelt, Theodore, 106

Sandburg, Carl, 18, 22, 34, 37–40, 58, 60, 67, 109, 113, 117; *Abraham Lincoln, The Prairie Years,* 104; "Chicago," 38; "Chicago Poems," 39, 71; "Grass, The," 109, 110; "To Webster Ford," 39, 60
Sangamon River, 4, 5, 10, 25, 35, 36, 110
Scanlon, Kicksham, 24, 25, 28
Scopes Trial, 14, 29, 102
Sexton, Anne, 122
Shelley, Percy Bysshe, 4, 12, 42, 47, 56, 63, 64, 66, 67, 102, 105
Sherman, Stuart Pratt, 76
Sinclair, Upton: *The Jungle,* 19
Spenser, Herbert, 14, 25
Spoon River, 5, 10, 25
Spiller, Robert E., 27
Stedman, E. C.: *American Anthology,* 63
Steinbeck, John: *The Pastures of Heaven,* 121
Sterling, George, 117, 121
Stevens, Wallace, 58
Stowe, Harriet Beecher: *Minister's Wooing, The,* 15; *Uncle Tom's Cabin,* 100, 119
Swedenborg, Emanuel, 102

Tennyson, Alfred, Lord: "Eagle, The," 66; *Idylls of the King,* 15; "Tears, Idle Tears," 66
Thomas, Dylan: *Under Milkwood,* 121

Thorp, Willard: *Literary History of the United States,* 119
Tietjens, Eunice, 41, 42, 68 *World at My Shoulder, The,* 42, 67, 74, 113, 114, 116
Tilbury Town, 30, 73; *See also* Robinson, A. E.
Twain, Mark, 2, *17–18,* 19, *81–82,* 106, *108–109; See also* Masters, E. L.: *Mark Twain: A Portrait; Adventures of Huckleberry Finn, The,* 6, 19; *Life on the Mississippi,* 17; *Tom Sawyer,* 16–18, *81–82,* 87, 88, 101

Villon, François, 63

Washington, George, 98, 102, 107
Whitman, Walt, 17, 59, 60, 62, 64, 66, 70, 71, 100, 105; *See also* Masters, E. L.: *Whitman; Leaves of Grass,* 16
Wilder, Thornton: *Our Town,* 121
Williams, William Carlos, 58, 120; *Book of Poems, A: Al Que Quiere!,* 71; *Paterson,* 122
Wilson, Lillian P., 80, 89, 95
Wordsworth, William, 64
World's Fair, Chicago. *See* Columbian Exposition
Wright, Willard Huntington, 61, 62

Yeats, William Butler, 116, 120
Yoknapatawpha County. *See* Faulkner, William